Peasant Revolts in China
1840–1949

Peasant Revolts in China
1840–1949

Jean Chesneaux

Translated by C. A. Curwen

W · W · Norton & Company · Inc

Picture Research: Célestine Dars

Printed and bound in Great Britain by Jarrold & Sons Ltd, Norwich

ISBN 0 393 05485 3 *(Cloth Edition)*
ISBN 0 393 09344 1 *(Paper Edition)*

Library of Congress Catalog Card Number: 72–13015

Contents

1 The Legacy of Peasant Rebellion in Pre-Modern China

Most of the great pre-industrial societies of the world have experienced explosions of 'peasant fury' and remember with fear and admiration such famous peasant rebels as Wat Tyler and the Lollards in England, the 'Jacques' of Beauvaisis and the 'Croquants' of Normandy, Stenka Razin and Pugachev in Russia, Thomas Münzer and his bands of starving peasants in Germany. But no country has had a richer and more continuous tradition of peasant rebellion than China.

Century after century, the long history of imperial China was punctuated by peasant revolts: the 'Yellow Turbans', the 'Red Eyebrows' and the 'Bronze Horses' at the beginning of our era, those against the Sung dynasty in the twelfth and thirteenth centuries and against the Ming in the seventeenth – to mention only the most important. The tradition was a rich one not only in the sense that peasant rebellions were frequent and often on a large scale, but also because it remained very much alive in the minds of the peasants of China in the nineteenth and twentieth centuries. It was not just an inert tradition from the dead past, but a dynamic element in living history, in the great waves of agrarian revolution which shook China from the middle of the nineteenth century onwards.

The peasant rebellions of ancient China have long been neglected by Western historians, who were themselves dependent upon traditional Chinese historiography which, as Etienne Balazs said, was 'written by scholar-officials for scholar-officials'. In the eyes of the mandarins, the defenders of the political order and of landed property, peasant rebels were no more than bandits. The Chinese term for them, *fei*, is an even more pejorative expression than its European equivalent. The 'bandit' is so named because a 'ban' has

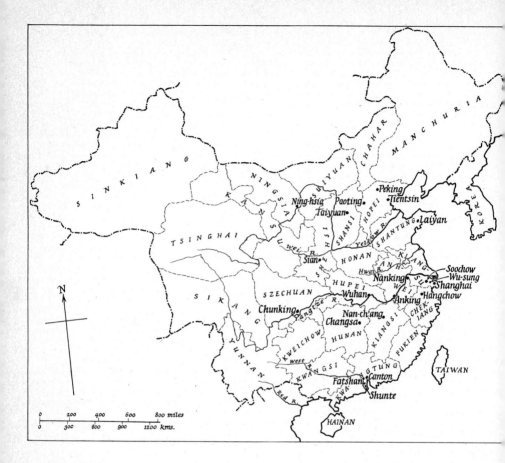

1 Map of China, showing the provincial boundaries and chief cities.

been pronounced against him, a sentence which isolates him from other men and makes him an outlaw. The Chinese term, however, denies him even the right to exist, since the character for *fei* is also a negative particle in classical Chinese grammar. Each man receives a name (*ming*) which defines his place in the social order; but the *fei* is one who does not exist in the eyes of good society. The historian does not need to know him, for he is concerned with the actions of the great and with the social structure which they created. This bias has survived for a long time among Western historians of China, who first discovered her history through the imperial annals, translated by the Jesuits in the seventeenth century. It is not without significance that one of the best known and best documented works of Western sinology dealing with the history of China between the mid-seventeenth century and 1911 is entitled *Eminent Chinese of the Ch'ing Period.*

Traditional Chinese historiography, based as it was upon Confucian political theory, tended to recognize the existence of peasant revolts only in cases where they succeeded in overthrowing one dynasty and founding another. Chinese society was founded upon respect for the established order, an order in which each man accepts his destiny and is content to exist only as a constituent element in a certain social system. Harmony between the social and cosmic orders is thus assured, and the Mandate of Heaven guarantees the overall harmony of the world. This harmony can be disrupted, however, and the emperor, the holder of the Mandate, may be proved unworthy. Removal of the Mandate from him (*ke-ming*) is announced by omens, by climatic disturbances, by corruption in the bureaucracy, by the degeneration of dikes and canals, and particularly by the growth of rural unrest. Such were the signs which foretold the fall of dynasties. Popular discontent might be powerful enough to bring about the downfall of an emperor and his evil ministers. Often it was the leader of peasant rebels who assumed imperial power and re-established Confucian legitimacy by means of popular rebellion. The traditional political order was sufficiently strong to reintegrate even its adversaries within its own system of thought, and assign them a role in the smooth functioning of society. Peasant revolts, far from threatening the principle of established order, are finally accepted as functional, as capable of restoring order in troubled times. They acted as safety-valves, able to restore to the world the benefits of the Heavenly Mandate.

One does not have to look far to find the reason for such frequent and dynamic peasant revolts as there were in ancient China; it existed in the bitter hardship of peasant life. Work on the land was meticulous, incredibly patient and skilful; it left profound traces of social activity upon the countryside particularly when, in order to meet the needs of rice cultivation, it involved irrigation and the preparation of perfectly level plots of land, often by means of terracing. Yet in spite of this, the Chinese peasantry never managed to conquer its natural environment: uncertain rainfall, recurring droughts, floods, typhoons, epidemics and locusts frequently caused poor harvests and famine.

Traditionally the peasants lived in village communities which still survived at the beginning of the twentieth century. Each community had its own elders, its own customs, fiscal and economic responsibilities – particularly for the organization of water resources – its festivals and its temples. The need of the peasants for communal structures is also shown by the vitality of clans, the members of which claimed common descent and had mutual rights and obligations. But these forms of peasant solidarity – the village, the clan and the family – were eroded by social differentiation within the villages themselves, by the antagonism between poor peasants and landlords. The land was very fragmented and cultivated in 'microfundia'. Ownership, however, was concentrated in the hands of rich families, who appropriated the major portion of what the peasants produced. Land rents, which commonly exceeded half the harvest, at a fixed or proportional rate, were collected in kind or in silver, and were supplemented by a whole series of customary dues and corvée exactions. The peasants were economically dependent upon the rich gentry, the 'masters of the land' (*ti-chu*). Even when a peasant was nominally owner of his own parcel of land, he was still dependent upon the landlord as his 'superior', as an arbitrator, as an intermediary with the fiscal and administrative authorities, and also as a money-lender. Rural society was not organized into great seignorial estates, like those of the Prussian junkers or the English squires, but the basic texture of society was the same. Even if the characteristic institutions of European feudalism, such as serfdom, were not present, the term 'feudalism' in its wider sense is not inappropriate. There was, nevertheless, a profound difference between Chinese feudalism and that of medieval Europe, not so much in the different ties of dependence imposed upon the peasants, but in the role of the state. In European feudalism the state had little significance and essential public functions were delegated to the lord. In China the state was all-powerful, and the peasant was as much exploited by the public demands of state and bureaucracy as he was by the individual greed of the landlord. In spite of the early appearance of private ownership of land, this socio-political structure, inherited from 'Asiatic' society, which Joseph Needham has aptly called 'bureaucratic feudalism', remained very stable.

The power of the Chinese ruling class was derived as much from its exercise of a social function as from its control of the land. The literati, or scholar-gentry, enjoyed a monopoly of education; they had the power of the state behind them, they imposed taxes (greatly to their own profit), administered justice and exercised control over the economy through the salt monopoly, by the supervision of taxation and markets, and by public works. Except in times of major dynastic crisis, the peasants were entirely excluded from participation in the affairs of the country. For the peasantry, the symbol and the centre of state power was the *yamen*, the office and residence of the local official and his subordinates. It was also the court of law, prison, barracks, arsenal and treasury, and, since taxes were usually collected in grain, a granary as well. In the Chinese countryside, the state *yamen* was the equivalent of the private feudal castle, a comparison which underlines the difference between Chinese and European feudalism. It was the *yamen* which the peasants sacked and burned when they rose up in rebellion.

The threefold subjection of the peasant – to nature, the landlord and the *yamen* – was further aggravated by the population explosion which took place in China after the end of the eighteenth century.

11

2 One clan family occupied this 'umbrella' house in Amoy as late as the first years of the twentieth century, evidence of the persistence of traditional clan structures.

In 1770 the population of China was 230 million; in 1830 it was 394 million. These are unreliable official figures, but they are enough to indicate the trend. Since the amount of cultivated land did not increase proportionally, large numbers of peasants were thrown off the land and forced into vagabondage. This marginal and restless section of the population played an almost negligible role in production except in so far as it provided a reserve of cheap labour; but it constituted a potential political force, the strength of which was considerable in times of trouble.

In a year when the harvest was bad, when a landlord was particularly rapacious or an official too authoritarian, there might be a revolt. The forms of agrarian struggle varied. Sometimes defiance would be individual, and a peasant would go off to join the bandits in the hills. Sometimes discontent would be widespread yet still limited to acts of defiance when it came to paying taxes or rents, or to minor incidents, such as a protest against a particular case of extortion. But in times of famine or economic crisis, real explosions of rebellion might occur, when the *yamen*, or even troops and convoys, were attacked, officials and landlords killed. Sometimes powerful undercurrents of unrest swelled into veritable peasant wars, lasting for several years and affecting entire provinces. Such were the rebellions of Fang La and Wang Hsiao-po at the end of the Sung dynasty and the rebellions at the end of the Ming, in the mid-seventeenth century.

The peasant risings of ancient China were fundamentally spontaneous, expressing a profound desperation and a confused search for a better life. It is possible, nevertheless, to trace a common historical denominator in the role of the secret societies, which provided them with a kind of ideology, with leaders and with a basic form of organization. Their ideology was egalitarian. A peasant rebel leader at the end of the T'ang dynasty (AD 618–906) announced himself to be 'the great general sent by Heaven to defend equality'. From what little the official chroniclers have seen fit to record, it is clear that the terms *t'ai-p'ing*, Great Peace, and *p'ing-chün*, Equality, appear again and again in the slogans and on the banners of peasant rebellions. They called for a violent struggle against the powerful, the rich and

3 A group of street beggars, a common sight in late nineteenth-century China.

the exploiters: 'When the officials oppress, let the people revolt!' – 'Attack the rich and help the poor!' The peasant ideology of revolt is full of religious feeling and nostalgia, looking back to a time of primitive justice, just as the Lollards in the fourteenth century or the Rhenish peasants of the sixteenth looked back to the days 'when Adam delved and Eve span'. The memory of past dynasties such as the Ming, the last national Chinese dynasty, was idealized, and in the nineteenth century its memory was revived in defiance of the Manchus who had overthrown it two centuries earlier. The religious element was expressed in the invocation of Heaven to restore justice, which showed the influence of Confucian ideas; but peasant revolts were above all fed by popular and dissident cults associated with Taoism and Buddhism. They were permeated by Buddhist millenarianism inspired by the Maitreya Buddha. For a time they were influenced by Manichaeism and exalted the principle of light against darkness. Chu Yuan-chang, the leader of a peasant rebellion against the Mongol Yuan dynasty in the fourteenth century, belonged to the White Lotus sect, of Manichaean origin, and the name of the new dynasty which he founded, the Ming (which means 'light' in Chinese), originated in the esoteric vocabulary of the Manichaeans.

The majority of peasant rebels were naturally recruited among the peasantry itself, but their leaders often came from other social strata. They might be ruined artisans from the margins of rural society, where men were more mobile than the peasants themselves because they were free from the servitude of the farming seasons and the day-to-day work on the land; Fang La, for instance, the leader of the great rebellion at the end of the Sung, was a bankrupt lacquer merchant. They might be stevedores, boatmen, pedlars or labourers; they might be *éléments déclassés* from the intelligentsia (what Frederic Wakeman calls 'lumpen-intelligentsia') – literati who failed the examinations, non-conformist or dissident intellectuals, Taoist or Buddhist monks, geomancers, itinerary medicine vendors, and so on. Some were even discontented members of the ruling class, 'black sheep' of respectable families, the ambitious and the adventurers, fond of intrigue and avid for notoriety.

Though the process of peasant revolt was by its very nature sporadic, the existence of the secret societies provided an element of continuity. It was from the secret societies that leaders emerged when there was a sudden outbreak of revolt, and they also served as refuges in case of defeat and in the interval between crises. Though these societies were not specifically peasant, they had many adherents among the urban poor, and they contributed greatly to the temporary successes of peasant revolts.

The innumerable secret societies of China fall broadly into two groups. The White Lotus and its affiliated societies, mainly in the north, including the 'Righteous and Harmonious Fists' (Boxers), the 'Big Sword Society', the 'Eight Trigrams', the 'Society of Observance' (*Tsai-li Hui*) and so on, were predominantly religious. The Triad system in the south was more political. It included the 'Society of Heaven and Earth' (*T'ien-ti Hui*), the 'Society of the Three Dots' (*San-tien Hui*) and the 'Society of the Three Harmonies' (*San-ho Hui*), which were probably different names for the same organization. The slogan of the Triads – 'Overthrow the Ch'ing and restore the Ming!' – has a distinctly national flavour: it called for an attack against the Manchus as foreign invaders. But it also implies a struggle against the imperial authorities as such. The Ming was a Chinese dynasty, but Ming loyalism was a kind of nostalgia, and part of the peasant and even of the millenarian tradition. The term '*hung-mi*', which means 'rice of the Ming', after the founder of the dynasty, and which frequently appears in the vocabulary of these secret societies, refers to the rice which will reward the faithful partisans of the fallen dynasty; but it is also the rice of 'abundance' (*hung*), the rice which will relieve the misery of the people.

Secret societies were directly involved in all the peasant rebellions in Chinese history. As early as the second century, the peasant war which overthrew the Han dynasty was led by a Taoist sect called the Yellow Turbans, whose esoteric canon was called the '*T'ai-p'ing-ching*' – the Classic of Great Peace. 'In peace time', declared a leader of the White Lotus when he was taken prisoner by imperial troops at the beginning of the nineteenth century, 'we preached that by reciting sutras and phrases one can escape the dangers of swords and arms, water and fire. . . . In time of confusion and rebellion we planned for greater enterprises.'

There were also other ways in which the secret societies responded to the needs and aspirations of the peasantry. They organized salt-smuggling against the state monopoly, for instance, allowing the peasants to procure salt at more reasonable prices. They acted as a kind of 'substitute lineage', which welcomed destitute peasants who had been deprived by their misery of family and descendants, freeing them from material and moral solitude, and replacing defunct families by an elective fraternity. The members commonly called each other 'brother' and one of the main secret societies of the nineteenth and twentieth centuries was called the 'Elder Brother Society' (*Ke-lao Hui*). They also acted as elementary mutual-aid groups, providing a measure of social security for their members, assisting families in case of sickness, disaster or death, welcoming travellers and giving protection of life and property. Finally, the secret societies welcomed women, whose lot was particularly hard in the Chinese countryside. In contrast to Confucian principles and custom, the secret societies asserted the equality of the sexes and often allowed women to achieve the highest ranks in their hierarchy. This primitive form of feminism can be seen in several of the peasant movements of modern China, including those of the Taipings and the Boxers.

Religious elements were always present in peasant rebellions, but their influence upon the secret societies was even more profound. Most of them practised esoteric cults, used initiation rites, trials by ordeal, mediums, charms which were supposed to give invulnerability and most promised their members the hope of spiritual salvation after death.

Without being a truly specific form of peasant movement – since they recruited members from other sections of the community in the countryside and especially in the towns – the secret societies added an element which made peasant revolts less spontaneous. They served to a certain extent as a catalyst of the peasant movement, giving it some form and modifying its intermittent and ephemeral character. In so far as one can speak of 'social consciousness' in the peasant movements of traditional China, it can have been no more than a very diffuse, vague sentiment. But there are signs that such a sentiment did exist, that the poor peasants of China were sometimes conscious of their collective identity and common destiny. This is expressed, for example, in a slogan which was common among the followers of the Triads in south China at the beginning of the nineteenth century:

> *The people of the top class owe us money,*
> *Those of the middle class should wake up.*
> *Lower classes come with us!*
> *It is better than hiring an ox to plough thin land!*

Popular ballads recited by itinerant singers, folksongs and folk tales were an important element in this peasant consciousness. Unfortunately these were purely oral forms of literature which the Confucian literati rarely deigned to record. Only after 1949, with the establishment of the People's Republic, did ethnographic and folklore teams penetrate into the furthest corners of the countryside in order to collect what might survive of this oral tradition, expressing the discontent and the struggle of the peasants. Enough was collected to fill several volumes.

In general, the research which they have undertaken in this veritable *terra incognita* of Chinese history – the Chinese peasant movement through the ages – represents the most original and solid achievement of the historians of People's China since 1949. Their work is inspired by the conviction of the Chinese Communists that they are the heirs to a long national tradition of peasant struggle. More than 400 works, books or articles, on this subject have been published in Peking or the provinces. References in the imperial annals or in local records, however brief, have been carefully collated and there have been many discussions between Marxist historians on several fundamental questions concerning the interpretation of peasant rebellions in traditional China. Some critics have denounced this as the 're-writing of history', an attempt to mould historical reality into a preconceived conceptual framework. But Chinese historians themselves differ on many fundamental points, such as the role of religion or of dissident members of the ruling class in these movements; and before deciding whether or not history has been 're-written' it would be as well to reach agreement on the necessity of writing this kind of history at all, on the value of exploring 'the other side of the river' after concentrating for so many centuries on the activities of the ruling classes.

Much of this unknown territory remains to be explored, and our understanding, even of that side of the river which belonged to the rich and powerful, is far from complete. Yet we can at least ask ourselves what historical role did peasant movements play in the evolution of imperial China through the ages? What function did they have in the dynamics of Chinese history?

In spite of their repeated failure, the peasant movements created an atmosphere of permanent insecurity, of social warfare. This is shown by the walls which both symbolically and functionally surrounded every Chinese town. These battlements existed, not because of the threat of foreign invasion – improbable in many parts of the country in view of their distance from the frontiers – but to defend the towns from attacks by peasants. The massive walls bear witness to the fact that the ruling class was never completely sure of its control over the countryside, and it is no accident, as we shall see later, that the Communist Party, which has most fully elaborated the theory of armed struggle as the way· to power, was formed and trained in a country where, for centuries, the peasants were accustomed to resist the ruling class by means of armed struggle.

The role of the peasant movements in China was not, however, merely a negative one. They attacked the established order, it is true, but again and again they sought to create a rebel order to put in its place, though we know very little about these efforts. At the end of the second century, for example, the Five Pecks of Rice sect, which rebelled against the later Han regime in the province of Szechuan under the leadership of Taoists, established in rebel territory 'inns of equality' (*i-shih*), where food was available free to passers-by. Similarly, in Sung times, rebels confiscated goods from the rich and organized their distribution to the poor peasant families. In 1643 Li Tzu-ch'eng, the leader of the rebellion which overthrew the Ming dynasty, proclaimed himself the 'King protected by Heaven', and with his peasant bands founded a rudimentary egalitarian and utopian state in north-west China, with communal administration of property. He gave administrative functions and grades to his followers and many members of the literati joined him and helped to draw up his proclamations.

The most important contribution of peasant movements in the historical play of forces in imperial China was in the overthrow of dynasties. The Ch'in regime (221–207 BC) was destroyed by peasant revolts; their leader Liu Pang proclaimed himself emperor and founded the former Han dynasty (206–23 BC). In their turn, the later Han (AD 25–220), the T'ang, and the Sung (AD 960–1279) were overthrown or irreparably weakened by great waves of peasant discontent. The Ming dynasty (1368–1644), which achieved power through popular revolts against the Mongols, was itself brought to an end by peasant rebellions under Chang Hsien-chung and Li Tzu-ch'eng, which were subsequently suppressed by the Manchus.

In the last analysis, peasant revolts served to confirm the Confucian theory of the Mandate of Heaven, consolidating the traditional political system by purging it when this became necessary. Their function as a built-in regulating mechanism in the ancient social and political system of the country is expressed in the well-known saying: 'He who fails becomes a bandit, he who succeeds – a king.' They never challenged more than the abuses of the traditional regimes: excessive taxation, the exactions of officials, the brutality of a land-lord, the neglect which led to disasters, and so on. They appealed to the Confucian principles of justice (*i*), the Way (*tao*) and the will of Heaven (*t'ien*).

There were several other factors which limited the actions of rebellious peasantry. Perhaps the most important one was the local-ized character of their activities, which reflected economic fragmen-tation and the restricted nature of the market. Their political horizons did not extend beyond the boundaries of the district in which the goods they produced or consumed were to be found. None of the innumerable rebellions of imperial China, however tenacious they may have been, affected more than a relatively limited geographical area: Szechuan in the case of the Five Pecks of Rice,

Shantung in the Fang La rebellion, the north-west in the case of Li Tzu-ch'eng, and so on. In the camp of the ruling class, on the other hand, if there was no economic basis for united action, there was nevertheless another kind of unity, which stemmed from that remarkable 'pan-Chinese' political force consisting of the gentry, the bureaucracy and the Confucian educational apparatus. In this sense there was a fundamental imbalance between the 'two sides of the river' – to the disadvantage of the peasants.

The sporadic, scattered and ephemeral character of peasant risings is also striking. They were discontinuous both in space and in time, for they were never more than the result of circumstantial conditions. They occurred again and again, but the rebels were never able to learn from their failures, to create a continuous strategy or open up new perspectives. All this underlines the inability of these peasant risings to free themselves from the historical fabric of ancient China.

Finally, the peasant movements were not able to escape another fundamental ambiguity, that between political revolt and criminality. In a political system such as existed in ancient China, where there was no machinery for the expression of political opposition (except in extreme cases when the removal of the Mandate of Heaven could give legitimacy to rebellion), opposition to the established order could never be less than total. A political dissident necessarily became a rebel, and resisted both the social and the moral rules of the system which he fought, including the rules of respect for human life and for other people's property – since peasant rebels, when supported by the masses, freely took the lives and goods of the rich and powerful. But in quiet times, when they were in retreat, they might on the other hand survive at the expense of 'good' peasants, and kill and ravage in the villages rather than in the *yamen*. The pull towards banditry within the peasant movement led straight to self-destruction. This, too, was an indication of its inability to free itself from the bourne of ancient China.

2 Peasant Rebellions in the Mid-Nineteenth Century

Partly as a result of the increase in population and a whole series of natural disasters, but above all because of a dynastic crisis of power, agrarian unrest, which had been muted in the seventeenth century, broke out again all over the country after the beginning of the nineteenth, with local incidents, secret society activities and armed risings. They were no more, however, than dispersed and marginal expressions of peasant discontent, and gave way, between 1850 and 1870, to a major wave of peasant rebellions of exceptional size. Several million peasants were involved; nearly all the eighteen provinces were affected; many of them, between 1855 and 1860, were totally or partially out of the control of the central government. Rebellions continued for almost twenty years, and constitute what was probably the greatest wave of peasant wars in history. But once more the rebellions of the Taipings, the Nien, the Moslems, and the risings led by the old secret societies, were separate movements, incapable of effectively coordinating their efforts. Consequently the Manchu dynasty was able, *in extremis*, to make an unexpected recovery.

It was no mere coincidence that this powerful peasant outburst occurred in the period of the Opium Wars and the 'opening' of China by the Western powers. The age-old contradictions between the peasants and the feudal holders of power, land and learning were deepened and brought to a climax by a combination of exceptional circumstances. The political and social crisis, which had been fermenting in the Chinese countryside since the beginning of the nineteenth century, was brutally exacerbated by the First Opium War and the Treaty of Nanking (1842). The Manchu dynasty was discredited by its readiness to give in to Western demands. The opium

4 Hung Hsiu-ch'üan (1814–64), mystic leader of the Taiping rebellion, an agrarian and nationalistic uprising against the Manchu dynasty.

traffic, illicit before the war, and then legalized, drained China of a large part of her reserves of silver, and changed, to the disadvantage of the peasants, the exchange rate between silver and copper. The opening of other ports in the east of the country deprived Canton of much of the commerce which had been concentrated there when it had been the only port open to foreign trade. Hundreds of thousands of boatmen and porters in central and southern China were thrown out of work, and it was from among this army of unemployed that several of the leaders of the Taiping rebellion emerged.

This most spectacular and exceptional of the great peasant movements of the mid-nineteenth century was more profoundly 'preconditioned' than peasant risings in general throughout the history of China. It occurred at the point when the traditional social crisis coincided with the penetration of China by the Western powers. This fusion of archaic and modern elements is shown in the geographical area where the movement originated and in the personality of its founder. Though Kwangsi may seem to have been no more than a typical province of old China, where for centuries peasants, gentry and secret societies confronted each other, it constituted the hinterland of Canton – the point of contact for more than a century between China and the West, the port frequented by Western merchants and missionaries. This influence was felt as far as Kwangsi. Hung Hsiu-ch'üan, the Taiping leader, shows the same combination of influences. He was an educated man from a family of poor peasants, who had not succeeded in gaining admission to the ranks of the ruling class. He had also been a pupil of a Protestant missionary in Canton. He had visited the great port and had experienced the historical 'gap' which existed between China and the 'barbarians'. In about 1845 Hung Hsiu-ch'üan began to preach a new faith in the mountains of Kwangsi. Into the 'Society of God-worshippers' which he formed, he welcomed landless peasants, coolies, miners, charcoal burners and disbanded soldiers. Initially his movement enjoyed the assistance of the Triad lodges which were very powerful in this area, and were the traditional meeting points for dissident elements. But he soon broke with the secret societies for ideological reasons: they refused to follow his attempted Christian syncretism. For his part, he disapproved of their dream of restoring the Ming dynasty, and in 1851 founded his own dynasty – 'The Celestial Kingdom of Great Peace' (*T'ai-ping T'ien-kuo*). Soon the Taiping armies, swelled by thousands of rebellious peasants, began their march to the northeast, and in 1853 arrived at Nanking, which remained the rebel capital for eleven years.

The Taiping movement was fundamentally an agrarian one, a revolt of the peasants against their 'natural' enemies within Chinese society, against landlords, gentry and officials. But at the same time it had a strong colouring of nationalism or proto-nationalism, and shows certain unique elements of modernization.

Its peasant character is reflected in the personality of its leaders, who gave themselves the archaic title of *wang* (king); many of them came from the poor peasantry of the south-west. As they advanced through central China and the Yangtze valley, the Taiping troops

5 A Taiping army moves into action, an illustration from Lin-le's record of the rebellion. Lin-le (an Englishman named Lindley) was one of the few Westerners

were supported by spontaneous peasant risings; officials, wealthy and unpopular landlords were put to death, tax registers, land registers and loan receipts were burned, government offices sacked. A contemporary chronicler wrote, 'Each time they entered into a rich house, or into that of a great family, they would dig three feet into the ground [to find buried treasure]. But not only did they not plunder the peasants, on the contrary, wherever they passed they distributed clothes and other things they had taken to the poor, and announced a remission of taxes for three years, thus winning the gratitude of the villagers.'

active in the Taiping cause; he was strongly critical of British intervention on behalf of the imperial forces.

In the same year that they set up their capital at Nanking, the Taipings promulgated their 'Land System of the Celestial Dynasty', the primitive collectivism of which places it in the direct tradition of Chinese peasant utopianism.

All lands under Heaven shall be farmed jointly by the people under Heaven. If the production of food is too small in one place, then move to another where it is more abundant. All lands under Heaven shall be accessible in time of abundance or famine. If there is a famine in one area move the surplus from an area where there

27

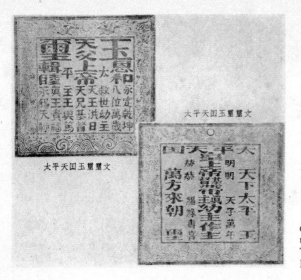

太平天囯玉璽璽文

太平天囯玉璽璽文

6, 7 Imprints of
the state seal of the
Taiping Heavenly
Kingdom.

is abundance to that area. . . . Land shall be farmed by all; rice,
eaten by all; clothes, worn by all; money, spent by all. There shall
be no inequality, and no person shall be without food or fuel. No
matter whether man or woman, everyone over sixteen years of
age shall receive land.

The same primitive collectivism, never widely enforced, however,
was to govern industrial production, by means of 'artisans' batta-
lions', the products of which went into 'state treasuries' and were
shared among all.

The elements of proto-nationalism in the Taiping movement
linked it with peasant revolts of the past, with the risings against
Mongol power in the fourteenth century, for instance, led by the
peasant Chu Yuan-chang, the founder of the Ming dynasty. The
Taipings wished to liberate China from the domination of the
Manchus. They accused the dynasty of being incapable of governing
China, of wanting to drain the country of its wealth, of being
responsible for the internal and external misfortunes of China.
Symbolically the Taipings cut off their queues, imposed upon the

Chinese in the seventeenth century as a sign of humiliation, and allowed their hair to grow – hence the contemporary epithet 'long-haired rebels' (ch'ang-mao tsei). This nationalistic element explains the recruitment by the Taipings of a number of educated and relatively wealthy people who had no particular reason to support the social struggle of the peasantry, but whose anti-Manchu patriotism gave them some sympathy for the rebel cause. They helped to draw up proclamations, undertook administrative functions, and made possible the creation of a real rebel state which survived for eleven years and controlled extensive territories.

The activities of the Taipings took place in a context which was no longer purely Chinese, for the shadow of the West had lain over China since the humiliating defeat in 1842. The Taipings were not indifferent to the challenge of the West; for instance, they adopted a semi-solar calendar in place of the old lunar calendar; they envisaged modern reforms, the construction of a network of railways, a postal service, hospitals and banks. Above all they attempted to penetrate the 'secret' of the Westerners in borrowing elements of their religion. They professed a militant monotheism; they accepted the Ten Commandments and the divinity of Christ, whose younger brother Hung Hsiu-ch'üan claimed to be; they practised baptism and gave the Old and New Testaments a place among their canonical books. These Christian elements were combined with popular traditional religions, with peasant cults and with Buddhist and Taoist elements. The Taipings thus created a complete politico-religious system, which combined spiritual salvation and obedience to the will of God with the political and military defence of the rebel state.

Like many other peasant rebels in history, the Taipings were subject to the contradictions inherent by definition in a rebel order. Should they be content with harassing the enemy, exposing its decadence, fighting and overthrowing the imperial regime, or should they, as others had done, attempt to construct new social machinery with its own forms of subordination and obligation? Could the revolt transform itself into a stable social structure without becoming a prisoner of the exigencies of such a structure? The Taipings began by conducting mobile warfare, all the way from the mountains of

Kwangsi to the city of Nanking. This was a real people's war, and the peasants rose in response. But once established in Nanking, the Taipings created the apparatus of government, with a capital, a political system, a bureaucratic administration and a group of leaders which soon became a privileged class. Many of the leaders had large harems, though in the army the Taipings preached monogamy and the separation of the sexes. To make this governmental machinery work involved increasing demands upon the peasantry, who ceased to be the motive force of a movement and became the subjects of a government. They had to pay taxes, suffer requisitions and give corvée services. This is why the peasantry became increasingly disaffected in the last years of the Celestial Kingdom of Great Peace. The rebel dynasty suffered the same withdrawal of allegiance in the rural areas under its control as had undermined the regime it sought to replace.

The disaffection of the peasantry, the main cause of the failure of the Taipings, was accompanied by certain other unfavourable factors. The movement never succeeded in controlling more than a fairly limited region. It was restricted in the first instance to the south-west, from which it detached itself soon after 1850, and then established more durable roots in Anhwei, Kiangsu and Chekiang in the lower Yangtze valley. Two expeditions against Peking, sent out in 1853 and 1854, did not succeed in mobilizing the peasants of the north and were utterly defeated. Moreover, the Taipings were weakened by dissension between ruling cliques. The two principal colleagues of Hung Hsiu-ch'üan, together with thousands of their followers, were killed in an outbreak of mutual slaughter in Nanking in 1856. Another gifted leader, Shih Ta-k'ai, preferred to flee Nanking with his troops and campaign on his own in the south-west. In 1859 the rebel king's cousin, Hung Jen-kan, a former catechist of Protestant missionaries in Canton and a capable administrator, arrived in Nanking. But he was soon ousted by powerful military men or incapable courtiers who had the fickle favour of Hung Hsiu-ch'üan.

In contrast to the weakening of the rebel regime, its enemy proved capable of vigorous recovery. From the beginning of the rebellion, imperial generals had been easily defeated. Since then, the gentry and

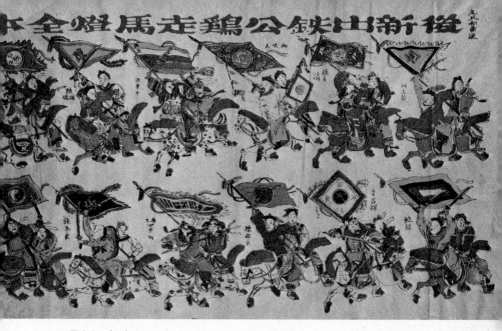

8 Taiping leaders, an idealized portrayal in a late nineteenth-century print.

landlords of the provinces had taken over the defence of their own economic interests. They organized disciplined and well-paid provincial militia and gradually established a blockade of rebel territory. The imperial government was also assisted in the reconquest of the empire by the Western powers, France and England, who, having once again imposed their will upon the Manchu dynasty in the Second Opium War and the Treaty of Tientsin (1858–60), preferred to maintain a conservative and docile government in Peking rather than see it swept away by rebels. Western aid, though not decisive, contributed to the defeat of the Taipings; Western officers helped to train imperial troops, steamships were put at their disposal for the transport of armies to the front in the lower Yangtze, foreign detachments sometimes even engaged directly in the hostilities and capable foreign officers, such as C. G. Gordon, commanded certain mixed units. Nanking was finally taken in the summer of 1864, and thousands of Taipings killed themselves with their leaders.

The peasant revolt of the Nien, which lasted from 1853 to 1868, took place in the sandy region of north China between the Yangtze

9 Imperial troops attack Nanking; on the battlements above the city's entrance Taiping leaders, among them Hung Hsiu-ch'üan, survey the battle. Nanking, Taiping capital from 1853 to 1864, finally fell to imperial troops, assisted by General Gordon, in September 1864, after a four months' siege.

basin and the Yellow River. It was less sophisticated than that of the Taipings and closer to the traditional model of peasant defiance.

This poor region north of the Hwai River was inhabited by robust and belligerent peasants. There were vast expanses of land unsuitable for rice cultivation and, exceptionally for China, there was an abundant supply of horses. Being close to the sea, there was a vigorous salt-smuggling trade, which provided a supplementary occupation for many people. Cart drivers and salt-smugglers played an important role in the Nien movement. In addition, this region was a kind of administrative no-man's land, overlapping parts of the provinces of Kiangsu, Honan, Shantung and Chihli – an 'under-administered' area far from the political centres and the bases from which repression was launched in the interior of each of these provinces.

The Nien, as a secret association of peasants, was possibly a branch of the White Lotus. The word Nien means a twist or roll, and was used to denote the cells of the organization, which became openly subversive in 1853, when the Taipings arrived at Nanking. The Nien benefited from the fact that the imperial forces were for several years preoccupied with the greater rebellion.

In the Hwai region there was little economic diversification, no large cities and few literati. The social composition of the Nien bands was consequently more homogeneous than that of the Taipings. Poor peasants predominated, and the recurrence of the same surnames in official government sources shows that whole villages and whole lineages rallied to the rebellion. The Nien behaved in much the same way as peasant rebels had done in preceding centuries: they attacked convoys of rich merchants, opened prisons, raided *yamen* and the houses of rich landlords. In the tradition of brigand justice they distributed goods to the poor and inscribed on their banners the words, 'Kill the officials, kill the rich, spare the poor!'

Peasant folksongs handed down for over a century, and recently collected by specialists in folk literature from Peking, reflect the class character of the Nien struggle:

> *As the moon goes round the sun,*
> *The poor rebel with the Nien.*
> *Poor turn to poor, rich to rich.*
> *As clearly different as black and white. . . .*

> *Shining red rises the sun;*
> *Lao-lo is a fine banner-leader.*
> *The poor men's hearts are happy to see him,*
> *And the moneybags' bones go soft with terror.*

> *. . . the paupers have overrun the whole land;*
> *as time goes by we'll see that you can do nothing.*

The fighting methods of the Nien armies were also much more in harmony with the peasant temperament than those of the Taipings,

10, 11 Two illustrations, taken from a Chinese picture book for children first published in 1963, show an imperial spy being arrested and summarily executed by Nien troops.

who quickly raised enormous armies of tens of thousands of men. The Nien, on the other hand, fought in small guerilla units, very mobile thanks to their horses, but still remaining close to the village population. Their code of conduct, forbidding looting or taking food from poor people, foreshadowed that of the Chinese Communists in the same region eighty years later, when their peasant guerillas and the Eighth Route Army were fighting the Japanese.

But the predominance of poor peasants in the ranks of the Nien did not preclude other elements from joining, such as salt-smugglers and 'black-sheep' from prosperous families. The chief leader of the Nien, Chang Lo-hsing, was himself a salt-smuggler.

The Nien organization was decentralized. Unlike the Taipings, they did not feel the need to establish a unified rebel state to challenge the imperial regime; at most their chiefs met in council to coordinate their actions. Nor did they attempt to win over the literati; they had

neither the need, nor the taste, for administrative red-tape or documents. Unlike the Taipings, they did not leave behind an imposing collection of edicts, canonical books or administrative statutes; so our knowledge of them is almost entirely based on what officials responsible for their suppression wrote about them. These sources nevertheless tell us something about their discipline, their dynamism, their fighting skill, the quality of their intelligence system, and about the support they enjoyed from the population. Such people as junior employees of the *yamen*, low-ranking officers in the imperial armies and merchants worked secretly for them and gave them immediate information about enemy troop movements.

The Nien movement is a typical example of what E.J. Hobsbawn has called 'social banditry'. But it also had a political character. A council of Nien chiefs, which met at Chih-ho in 1856, adopted anti-Manchu, anti-dynastic proclamations and called upon their followers to fight for the 'Great Han Kingdom' – for a Chinese dynasty as opposed to the 'barbarian' regime of the Manchus. Chang Lo-hsing, the former salt-smuggler, was nominated 'Great Han Prince with the Ming Mandate'. It is clear that the Nien movement was influenced by Ming loyalism and anti-Manchu proto-nationalism. In engaging in salt-smuggling on a grand scale and setting up its own inland customs posts, it fought against the monopolies of the imperial state, supplanting them and encouraging the development of local commerce.

The history of the Nien movement can be divided into three phases. Until 1855 they were assembling and consolidating their forces. Then, until 1864, they profited from the existence of the Taiping regime to the south of them and cooperated militarily with it. But after the defeat of the Taipings in 1864 the imperial forces turned their attention to the Nien who, reinforced by Taiping survivors, continued vigorous resistance against the government. In 1865 they defeated and killed the government's best general, the Mongol cavalry commander Seng-ko-lin-ch'in. With their mobile guerilla bands they were still a powerful fighting force, and campaigned over much of north China. Unlike the Taipings, their relations with the peasants and with the villages remained excellent. But their very success, the fact that they survived for fifteen years, accelerated their downfall. In 1867 they chose to organize great regiments, as the Taipings had done. The 'Eastern Nien' moved into Shantung while the 'Western Nien' sought to join up with the Moslem rebels who were then at the height of their activity in the north-west. From now on, the Nien were much more vulnerable and could no longer melt away into the villages as they had previously done in times of danger. The two great armies were encircled, divided and wiped out, and the movement came to an end in 1868.

Apart from the major rebellions of the Taipings and the Nien, Chinese peasants took part in many other movements against the established order in the third quarter of the nineteenth century. The great Moslem rebellions of Yunnan (1853–73) and north-west China

12 Official seal of Tu Wen-hsiu, leader of the rebel Moslem forces in Yunnan; the inscriptions are in Arabic (left) and Chinese.

(1863–73) were ethnic and religious in character, but their social base was nevertheless a peasant one. The same is true of the rebellion of the Miao minority in the province of Kweichow (1854–72). In these regions inhabited by minority peoples, ethnic antagonism did not replace poor peasant opposition to the landlord-official alliance, but exacerbated it. The peasants of these minorities paid their Chinese landlords rents which were even higher than in the rest of China, and suffered treatment at the hands of officials which was even more severe. They were also exploited by Chinese merchants who sold them necessities such as tea and salt at high prices, but gave them little for their goods, such as furs, wool and the products of the forests, which were much in demand elsewhere.

The secret societies had supported the Taiping rebellion only at the beginning; their influence upon the Nien was remote. In spite of certain similarities, the Nien did not constitute a secret society in the strict sense of the term. But these ancient subversive groups took advantage of the weakening of central power to organize a whole series of minor risings, very scattered to be sure, but which in fact involved as many peasants as the Taipings and the Nien. In Szechuan, for instance, about 1860, the Red Band (*Hung-pang*) led a revolt of more than 30,000 peasants. The Red Turban rebellion of Canton (1854), led by the Triads, involved peasants, smugglers, vagabonds and bandits. The peasants of the Canton region sought the support of the secret societies against the officials and landlords; they formed village defence corps and practised the art of Chinese boxing. Once the Triads succeeded in coordinating the actions of the peasant bands of the plain with those of the 'professional'·outlaws from the mountains, the rebel force was strong enough to lay siege to important market towns near Canton. Fatshan and Shunte were even occupied for a time, but the rebels were not able to hold them for more than a few weeks.

In spite of a crisis lasting twenty years, the imperial government was able to survive all these major and minor rebellions. There had been occasional attempts at strategic cooperation among the rebels; the Taipings had campaigned with the Nien and had contact with the Moslems and even certain secret societies towards the end, but there was never any real coordination between the rebel forces. Indeed it was impossible; it would have made no sense in the historical context of the traditional Chinese order. All the peasant movements and secret society risings between 1850 and 1870, all expressions of peasant violence, were the result of local conditions and circumstances. By their very nature, they each presented a different social and ideological profile, out of which it was not possible to create a 'united front'. The Ming loyalism of the secret societies could not be reconciled with the claims of the rebel 'Celestial Kingdom' at Nanking, nor did the Nien have the same motives and perspectives as the Moslem peasants.

The forces of suppression triumphed in the end, but at the cost of tremendous slaughter. Even in the middle of the twentieth century, cities such as Nanking and Soochow, the main urban bases of the

Taipings and until then flourishing centres of commerce and manufacture, still showed traces of the destruction which had occurred when they were recaptured by the imperial forces. In the countryside the effects of suppression were even more brutal. Certain provinces, according to the most recent Chinese census (1953), had not yet recovered, a century later, from that terrible bloodletting. The victims of these great peasant risings, and above all of the process of suppression which finally brought them to an end, have been estimated in tens of millions.

3 The Chinese Peasantry and the Collapse of the Imperial Order

During the last thirty years of the nineteenth century, there was a general ebb in the Chinese peasant movement. The great storms of the 'fifties and 'sixties had subsided, and the vitality of the peasantry had been seriously weakened by defeat and suppression. The imperial regime, on the other hand, emerged strengthened from the ordeal. The provincial gentry, the traditional adversaries of the peasants, had profited from the crisis not only to take in hand the protection of their own privileges on the local level and the struggle against the rebels, but had also forced their services upon the Manchus. Important Chinese landlords of central China who had defeated the Taipings, such as Tseng Kuo-fan and Tso Tsung-t'ang, now had considerable power in Peking and had the confidence of the Dowager Empress Tzu-hsi. They hoped to put China on the 'Japanese road', by combining conservative political and social policies with limited modernization in technical and intellectual fields. This was the 'foreign matters' (*yang-wu*) movement, which sought to manage the affairs of China in a Western manner.

The new conditions established in the Chinese countryside after the suppression of the rebellions also placed the peasants in an unfavourable position. Because of the immense bloodletting which had taken place (70 per cent of the population of Anhwei, for example, had perished), there were great movements of population that brought temporary disruption to peasant communities or what remained of them. Millions of peasants came from such regions as Hunan or Fukien to settle in the devastated areas. The newcomers were treated with distrust by the survivors of the old population, and peasant solidarity against the oppression of officials and landlords was weakened by this influx of displaced persons. The re-establishment of imperial authority in the rebel zones was conducted with solemnity, in order to impress upon the peasants that the victorious gentry could no longer be defied. A mass movement like those of the 1850s was now inconceivable.

On the other hand, this disruption of rural society, by its very depth, played into the hands of the secret societies, because newly arrived peasants, placed suddenly in a hostile environment, had nowhere else to turn for a measure of security. The influence of the secret societies also grew among those soldiers who, demobilized as soon as their task of suppression had been accomplished, often found themselves hundreds of miles from home and were rapidly reduced to vagrancy or banditry. The first effects of technological modernization also brought new recruits to the secret societies. Steamships, which had become a common sight on the Yangtze and along the coasts, reduced thousands of boatmen, porters and stevedores to unemployment. They, too, could turn to the secret societies, particularly to the Elder Brother Society (*Ke-lao Hui*) or to the Society for Men of Rivers and Lakes (*Chiang-hu Hui*), which consisted of pirates. It was no coincidence that the area where the Elder Brother Society was most active in the last three decades of the nineteenth century was the lower and middle reaches of the Yangtze. This was the scene of the final suppression of the Taipings, where the number of disbanded soldiery was greatest and where steam navigation was rapidly developing.

For a time, new conditions prevented the upsurge of a fresh wave of peasant unrest and limited it to more spontaneous, fragmented forms of expression, through the secret societies, for instance. Yet the latter emerged, paradoxically, strengthened by the crisis, and were to play an important role in the upsurge of the peasant movement which was to come.

Their defeat had done nothing to ameliorate the peasants' misery; elementary protests and riots continued. Peasants might refuse to pay rents or manhandle the landlords' agents. Minor or localized incidents might occur when extortion or the greed of officials became unbearable. In north China an incident was provoked by the unjust financial manipulations of a local official. The revenue of the peasants was in strings of copper cash, whereas the taxes were collected in silver, and the exchange rate was fixed by the authorities. In this particular region, some time between 1880 and 1890, the rate jumped from 2,000 copper cash per *tael* of silver to 8,000, for no other reason than the desire for illicit gain. This meant that the taxes were effectively quadrupled.

These incidents and spontaneous commotions were often no more than a tragic and spectacular form of collective suicide. Marshal Chu Te, who was born in Szechuan in 1886 in a family of poor peasants, recalled one of the first memories of his infancy. A famine was raging and the family of Lord Ting, a rich landlord, kept jealous watch over his riches –

[I] heard a strange sound. . . . A horseman galloped wildly down the road and on toward the Ting home, and the strange sound grew louder, coming from the north where a cloud of dust was rising along the Big Road.

From the dust cloud there soon emerged a mass of human skeletons, the men armed with every kind of weapon, foot-bound women carrying babies on their backs, and naked children with enormous stomachs and cavernous red eyes plodding wearily behind. Through a vast confusion of muttering voices, [I] heard the urgent clanging of cymbals and the roll of drums from the Ting mansion. The King of Hell [Ting's nickname] was summoning his tenants to fight for him.

The men of the Chu family heard the summons but did not move. The avalanche of starving people poured down the Big Road, hundreds of them eddying into the Chu courtyard, saying: 'Come and eat off the big houses!'

Grandfather and grandmother Chu laid restraining hands on their sons. . . . Then the 'hunger marchers' were gone. The Chu family was not yet desperate enough to join them. . . . A few nights later, desperate peasants took refuge in the Chu home and talked in whispers of a wild battle in which hundreds of starving people had been killed, wounded or taken prisoner. They had fought fiercely, and had taken many soldiers with them into the

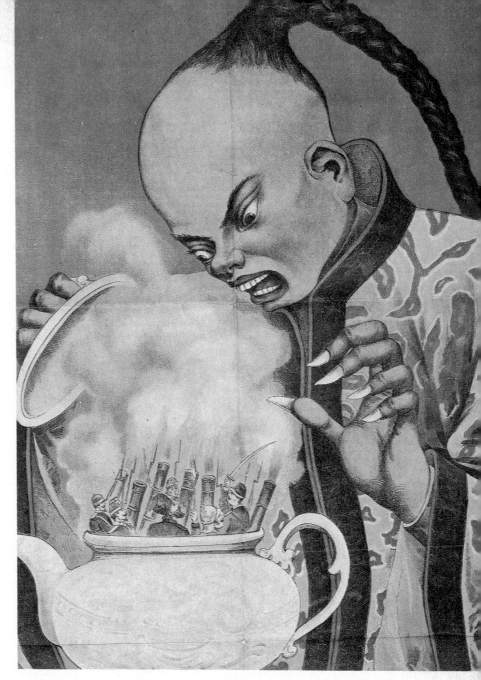

13 *The Miracle Teapot*, a malicious Russian cartoon of Chinese reaction to Western interventionist policies; within the pot, and ready for action, are soldiers from Germany, Russia, England, France, America and Japan.

shadows. Before the soldiers had caught up with them they had besieged the Ting estate and other big family homes, and though some had been killed they had entered and eaten.

Such an atmosphere of misery and despair, together with the memory of the disappointed hopes which had inspired the Taipings and the Nien, favoured the growth of secret society activity. Thousands of these subversive groups were active in the last three decades of the nineteenth century; they were swelled by increasing numbers of *éléments déclassés* and discontented people of all kinds. Some of the societies were very powerful, such as the Triads or the Elder Brother Society (*Ke-lao Hui*) which stemmed from it; others were very small, such as the small peasant fraternities of Hunan and Shantung, called *fu-tang* (Turban Gangs). Whether large or small, they had the same ancient slogans as before: 'Kill the rich and help the poor!', 'Restore justice in the name of Heaven!', 'Overthrow the Ch'ing and restore the Ming!' Tirelessly they organized revolts, but these were both ephemeral and localized. The following chart, made by the Chinese historian, Wang T'ien-chiang, from what was certainly an incomplete survey, gives an idea of the distribution of these revolts throughout the country:

	1860–70	1870–85	1885–95
Hunan	27	25	3
Kiangsi	6	4	3
Hupei	7	7	1
Kweichow	–	6	1
Kwangtung	–	4	2
Honan	2	3	2
Anhwei	–	–	1
Yunnan	–	1	3
Kwangsi	–	1	6

The collapse of the Manchu dynasty in 1911 was not the result of an ordinary dynastic crisis, such as that which had put an end to the Ming dynasty in the seventeenth century or the Yuan in the fourteenth. For the first time in the history of China, the imperial system itself foundered with the falling dynasty. The unprecedented scale of this disintegration was due to the fact that the traditional factors which heralded the fall of dynasties (corruption and the negligence of officials, natural calamities, agrarian unrest, neglect of public works) were now accompanied by other factors, due to the accelerated penetration of the West. Since the middle of the nineteenth century, the traditional equilibrium of Chinese society had been increasingly disturbed. It had been shaken by the consequences of the unequal treaties, by capitalist economic penetration and, since 1895–1900, by the effects of what was called the 'break-up' of China – the opening of mining and railway concessions demanded by the foreigners, financial subordination to great foreign banks and the allocation of zones of influence to the Western powers. The *Ancien Régime* of China was incapable of resisting the pressures of imperialism; it could do no more than attempt a solution to the kinds of problems dealt with in the conservative and limited modernization policies of the 'foreign matters' period.

Weakened by these external pressures, the empire was also threatened by the actions of new social groups, a new intelligentsia and a new commercial bourgeoisie born out of the collision with the West. Unlike what had happened in previous dynastic crises, the traditional order found itself under attack from external forces which it had not created. Since the end of the nineteenth century the radical republicans, representing the new social classes (including a young military intelligentsia, as modern as the new intellectuals themselves), had begun to form vigorous clandestine groups. They succeeded after many set-backs in taking power in 1911, though in a very fleeting manner. The most active and best-known of these groups was Sun Yat-sen's T'ung-meng Hui (United League), which later became the Kuomintang.

The ancient Chinese empire succumbed to a threefold pressure: foreign penetration, the traditional mechanism of social and political crisis, and the activity of modern revolutionaries. The peasants, forming the mass of the Chinese population, were directly concerned in these processes. They reacted violently to foreign penetration, they participated vigorously in the general movement of revolt against

45

14, 15 Two popular anti-Christian and anti-Western woodcuts, made in the early 1890s. Left, *The God of Thunder Destroying the Pigs and the Goat*; the goat represents the Great West (*Ta-hsi*) and the pigs Jesus (*Ye-su*) and his disciples (*Chiao-t'u*). The more specifically anti-Christian *Shooting the Pig and Decapitating the Sheep*, right, portrays Jesus as a pig and his disciples as sheep.

the Manchu dynasty, and they cooperated with the new adversaries of the established order – the republican conspirators.

The peasants reacted against foreign penetration, but they could do so only in so far as it was perceptible to them. They had no knowledge, or very little, of what went on in treaty ports such as Shanghai, Tientsin or Wuhan, which were the nerve centres of Western penetration, with their concessions, the consular courts, newspapers, presses, mission headquarters, universities, banks, factories, docks, steamship companies, garrisons and so on. Only marginal or episodic aspects of this Western domination reached as

46

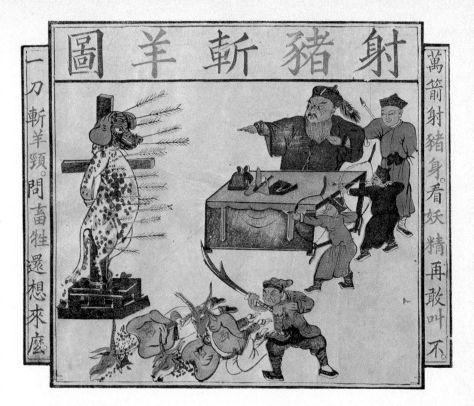

far as the Chinese countryside – perhaps a military expedition, some aspect or result of industrialization, and especially the activities of Catholic or Protestant missionaries. Peasant resistance to foreign enterprises was at this stage confined to specific events and circumstances. Only in the twentieth century, and only after Japanese troops began to penetrate the Chinese countryside, was the peasantry capable of carrying out a meaningful struggle for the national salvation of China.

In the nineteenth century there were only isolated cases of peasant opposition to foreign armies; the forces of the West or of Japan had not yet been obliged to campaign for prolonged periods in the vast interior of the country. The wars of 1839–42, 1856–58, 1884–85, 1894–95

47

16 Name-plate of the Mining Department of the Shantung Railway Company, established by Germany in 1898 when she was granted the exclusive right to develop Shantung's mineral resources.

17 Military presence: American police-station in Peking, 1902. American forces were part of the international expedition sent to quell the Boxer Uprising in 1900: a garrison remained to protect the embassy.

18 Classical Western architecture in a Chinese setting: the British Factory at Canton, 1843.

19 Missionary presence: Deaconess Ellen Mort, an Australian missionary active in Fukien between 1898 and 1904, prepares to start her rounds.

had been resolved by the hasty capitulation of Peking. The peasants, whose military effectiveness in resistance was to prove so decisive in defeating Japan, had so far had little opportunity to show their strength, except in brief and rare episodes. In 1841, at San-yuan-li, a suburb of Canton, villagers routed a detachment of Anglo-Indian troops. In 1884–85 the Black Flags of Tonking and the border regions of south China had offered sturdy resistance against French troops. They were half peasant, half mercenary, but inspired by a primitive and vigorous proto-nationalism. The Hung-hu-tzu (Red Beards), mounted bandits of Manchuria, had also effectively opposed Russian penetration into that region during the construction of the Transmanchurian Railway, and armies had to be brought up before they could be suppressed.

Equally fragmentary and scattered was peasant resistance to the penetration of Western techniques and Western capitalist economy. As so often happens in the first phases of industrialization, it took the form of machine-breaking. But Chinese 'luddism' was not motivated by purely economic aims, like that which appeared at the beginning of the nineteenth century in England; it also had political motives of a nationalistic kind. Modern techniques were refused because they were foreign, and not just because they were causes of unemployment. Modern machines for the spinning and weaving of silk, for example, were destroyed in the rural districts near Canton in the 1880s. The best-known case is that of the railway between Wu-sung and Shanghai, constructed in 1875 and demolished two years later after a mass rising of peasants in the region, supported by local gentry. Railways were said to disturb the tombs in the fields, to annoy the spirits and violate the laws of geomancy (*feng-shui*). Peasant resistance against modern industrial technology continued in the towns, to which their misery had driven them in search of work in the factories. At the end of the nineteenth century and the beginning of the twentieth, there were many cases of factory-smashing (*ta-ch'ang*). These were workers' riots in which erstwhile peasants, unused to the atmosphere of the towns and suffocating in the factories, became desperate and took to smashing all the modern machinery.

The only close and long-term contact Chinese peasants had with the West was with the missions. Relations were very bad. The peasants loathed the new Chinese converts, or 'rice Christians', who were accused of seeking a cheap means of protection against the Chinese authorities in case of trouble with the police or with the law, and as a kind of insurance against misery. The missions were accused, and particularly the Catholic orphanages, of kidnapping children. The choice of sites for churches and missions was objectionable, often contravening the rules of *feng-shui*, which the missionaries naturally considered as a part of 'pagan superstition' and were only too glad to defy.

After 1860 there was an increasing number of incidents involving missionaries, attacks on mission buildings, the destruction of churches and chapels, manhandling of Chinese converts and so on. In 1891 a series of anti-Christian riots broke out in several small towns and rural markets in the Yangtze valley. At I-ch'ang on 2 September 1891 a crowd burned the American Protestant church, the British Consulate and the residence of the English Inspector of Customs, part of the Imperial Maritime Customs which covered the whole country, even at this distance from the sea. These were movements of both the peasantry and the urban poor; but local gentry, as they had done in the case of the Wu-sung railway and in the San-yuan-li incident, supported and even incited the peasants against the foreigners, distributing placards and lampoons, furnishing arms and organizing popular discontent. In some cases the secret societies – traditional enemies of the gentry – were also mixed up in these anti-Christian outbreaks. The Elder Brother Society, for example, was probably behind the incidents of September 1891.

The Boxer Uprising (1897–1900) was the climax of all these trends, of peasant hostility to Christianity on religious grounds, of popular proto-nationalism, of secret society activity, of 'luddite' resistance to modern technology, and also of the traditionalist, anti-Western feeling of the local gentry.

The movement started in a peasant secret society, the Band of Right and Harmony (*I-ho T'uan*), probably connected with the White Lotus, in the provinces of Chihli and Shantung. The peasantry of north China had suffered serious agricultural disasters, famines in 1896–97 and floods of the Yellow River in 1898. Boatmen on the Grand Canal had been ruined by the spread of steam navigation. The concessions obtained by foreigners after the 'break-up' of China, following her defeat at the hands of Japan, caused great public indignation, particularly the encroachment of Germany in the province of Shantung, which had been recognized as a German 'sphere of influence'. In origin the movement was both anti-foreign and anti-dynastic, attacking the missions and at the same time invoking the name of the Ming dynasty in the tradition of the White Lotus.

The revolt also had a religious character. The Boxers practised oath-taking, esoteric boxing and the use of charms which were supposed to give invulnerability. They harked back to a primitive millenarianism which announced the imminent arrival of 'the ten calamities'. But the movement was above all a political one, inspired by elementary nationalism – 'Exterminate the foreigners' was inscribed on its banners. Economic elements were also present: the Boxers attacked railways which were under construction, telegraph lines, etc.

There was hardly any central command in the Boxer movement, only basic units called 'altars' (t'an), consisting of supporters from one or more villages. There were special groups of young boys – who were among the most fanatical – and of women, whose groups went by the name of 'green lanterns' or 'red lanterns'. The existence of secret societies consisting only of women is probably a sign of the acuteness of the social crisis and the decline of the family tradition even in the countryside. The women's units of the Boxers were not the only examples of this. In south China at this time there were clandestine associations of unmarried women thieves.

It is also worthy of note that the area affected by Boxer activities was fairly narrowly limited to the provinces of Chihli and Shantung. Movements of the same name flared up in Manchuria and in Shantung, but at a later date and apparently on local initiative.

Originally anti-dynastic, the Boxers gradually accepted a kind of official recognition: the Manchus hoped to use them to halt foreign

20, 21 Two Boxer banners: top, a dragon-pearl design, originating in T'ang legend; the slogan on the banner on the left reads 'Support the Ch'ing, destroy the foreigner!'

22 Right, a Boxer soldier, an illustration from a Chinese textbook published in 1964.

23 Peasant discontent, born of famine and poor harvests, led
to frequent rioting in the early years of the twentieth century:
this contemporary woodcut, *The Starving People Seize the Grain*,
shows hungry peasants attacking a landlord.

demands for concessions. The conservative gentry were not ignorant of this *rapprochement*, and the new slogan of the Boxers became 'Support the Ch'ing and eliminate the foreigners' (*fu-Ch'ing mieh-yang*). In 1900, when the Manchu court fled to the north-western city of Sian, the Boxers occupied Peking and laid siege to the foreign legations, providing the pretext for the launching of an international expedition by the Western powers, which brought the uprising to an end.

The Boxer affair was not a peasant movement in the full sense of the term, since attention was concentrated on resistance to foreign encroachment and the activity of the missions. The Boxers' para-doxical collusion with the gentry shows them to have been conser-vative as regards internal politics; they were content with no more than a vague slogan about 'protecting the people'. They had nothing like the dynamism of the Nien, who had been active in the same region thirty years earlier. Nevertheless, their social base was genuinely a peasant one, even if some of their militants and leaders, such as ruined bargeowners and disbanded soldiers, came from other social strata. They expressed the indignation of the peasantry at foreign encroachment, even if the priority which they gave to this problem prevented them from expressing traditional peasant hostility towards the established regime. In fact, they contributed by the vigour of their movement to hastening the fall of the Manchu dynasty, which they had considered as a possible tactical ally against the foreigners.

Even after 1902, in the province of Chihli, there was an armed assembly of 150,000 peasants, who formed 'village leagues' to protest against the indemnity which the Chinese government had agreed to pay the Western powers and the missionaries after the uprising. The indemnity had brought about fiscal difficulties, the burden of which fell, as usual, on the peasants.

The totality of Ch'ing imperial policy in the first years of the twentieth century aggravated the misery of the peasants. The Manchu government wanted to maintain the traditional political and social structures, and at the same time to play the game of modernization – with loans from abroad, railway construction, factories and arsenals, a new army, administrative reforms, abolition of the Confucian examination system and the establishment of modern schools. State expenditure was considerably increased by these measures, though the resources available were those of a pre-industrial economy and an archaic fiscal system. In the last analysis, since the rich revenues of the customs were directly appropriated by the foreigners, it was the taxes paid by the peasants which financed the administration and produced a surplus. Consequently taxes proliferated at the slightest pretext in order to pay for this or that reform, debt or indemnity.

Peasant discontent, very episodic and scattered in the last part of the nineteenth century, took on a new vigour. Risings broke out in Kwangsi between 1900 and 1906 under Triad banners, and in Szechuan under those of the Boxers. In Kiangsi in 1904 there was a riot against a new tax on indigo, theoretically intended to finance a new education programme. Indigo was the main industrial crop of the peasants in this region, their main means of livelihood. The rioters destroyed the tax bureaux and the Catholic church, among other things.

Riots were frequent in the period immediately before the republican revolution. A survey made at the time by the pioneer Shanghai journal, *Tung-fang Tsa-chih* (Eastern Miscellany), counted 113 peasant riots in 1909 and 285 in 1910. Intensification of peasant unrest was often connected with natural disasters; for instance, the harvests had been very bad in 1909–10. In general, however, it was a sign that the prestige of the dynasty was declining rapidly, and of the widespread belief that there was to be a rupture of the Mandate of Heaven (*ke-ming*). Other riots between 1909 and 1911 were caused by the increase in the price of salt, the production and distribution of which was a state monopoly; by famine and the scarcity of rice, as in the rice-riots of Changsha, the capital of Hunan, in May 1911; by new taxes on grain, and by the multifarious taxes imposed by the Manchu authorities *in extremis* to pay for urgent reforms. At Laiyang in Shantung, for example, riots broke out in June 1910 against excessive taxation, and a whole district revolted. Troops had to be called in and the revolt was suppressed at the cost of 40,000 lives.

This new wave of popular discontent, of primitive peasant riots, undoubtedly contributed as much to the fall of the dynasty as did the determined underground work of the militant republicans. But only the latter were organized, only they had a political programme and a concept of historical progress. Peasant risings in many parts of the country between 1909 and 1911 nevertheless played an essential role, creating a political and ideological vacuum, showing the isolation of the Manchus and the imminence of their fall, and confirming that the tenacity of the republicans was historically justified.

Nor were the republicans indifferent to this wave of peasant unrest. Most of them were intellectuals, officers in the new armies and members of the liberal professions. Most came from gentry families or the urban bourgeoisie, though a few, including Sun Yat-sen himself, were of peasant origin. They were conscious of the narrowness of their social base and of their relative isolation within Chinese society, and of the need for the support of the peasant masses in the struggle against the imperial regime. For this reason they gave a place in their political programme to agrarian questions and sought military and political cooperation with the secret societies.

Sun Yat-sen was born in a family of poor peasants in Kwangtung and liked to call himself the son of a 'coolie', though in fact, having a brother who was a rich planter in Hawaii, and himself a doctor graduated from a British medical school in Hong Kong, he belonged more to the new bourgeois intelligentsia. The programme which his T'ung-meng Hui adopted consisted of three points: the sovereignty of the people - democracy; the independence of the people - national liberation by the overthrow of the Manchu dynasty; and 'the livelihood of the people'. The third principle was deliberately vague and he interpreted it, in 1924 for instance, in a socialist sense in order to please his left-wing allies. It could, on the other hand, be presented as a 'Chinese solution', which might be the basis of a social-democratic, Western-style economy.

Among the measures which Sun Yat-sen envisaged for the achievement of 'people's livelihood' was 'equalization of land rights'. The formula was imprecise, bearing little resemblance to a genuine land distribution programme; it meant little more than giving the state

24 Sun Yat-sen (1866–1925), appointed first President of the Republic of China in 1912.

the right to appropriate surplus land. A general evaluation of land values was to be carried out first and the state would have the perpetual right of pre-emption and could buy back land at this basic price, or could withhold the surplus realized by a private vendor. Sun Yat-sen's system had been inspired by the ideas of the American economist, Henry George, a vague liberal socialist whom he greatly admired; but it showed, by the use of the term 'equalization' (*p'ing-chün*), the influence of the egalitarian, utopian tradition of the past – a theme evoked again and again by heterodox literati and peasant rebels. Sun Yat-sen's use of this expression was a harking back to the tradition of Chinese agrarian struggles, although the theoretical implications of the proposed reform stemmed more from capitalist economic principles and had little meaning for the mass of Chinese peasants.

To mobilize the peasants in active struggle against the Manchu regime more was needed; appeals had to be made directly to their traditional representatives – the secret societies. Many of the republican leaders, particularly those close to Sun Yat-sen, were members of the Triad or the Elder Brother Society, and it was easy for them to make contact with the rural lodges of these societies. Chu Te relates in his memoirs how he joined the Elder Brother Society when he was an officer in the New Army, in order to establish contact with simple soldiers of peasant origin. Certain secret society leaders, for their part, made approaches to the radicals. In Hunan, for example, in about 1905, a poor peasant called Ma Fu-i, who was at the head of a Triad lodge and had considerable popular prestige, was contacted by Huang Hsing as one of the chief republican leaders. They even planned a joint military action, but their efforts were frustrated by the arrest and execution of Ma Fu-i.

The idea of strategic cooperation and joint military operations between republican groups and the secret societies was in the air. When the republicans planned to seize the provincial *yamen* in Canton they appealed to local Triad groups, who participated in the abortive attack. At the end of 1906 an ambitious plan was made for large-scale military operations in the districts of P'ing-shan, Liu-ling and Li-ling, on the border regions of Hunan and Kiangsi. This insurrection was carried out as part of the T'ung-meng Hui programme of activity, and lasted until the beginning of 1907. The traditional guerilla tactics of the peasants proved very successful and more than ten thousand troops had to be called in before it was suppressed.

The same year, one of the main leaders of the republicans, Sung Chiao-jen, made a journey to Manchuria and established contact with thirty-six peasant-bandit chiefs of the Hung-hu-tzu (Red Beards). The mobilization of 100,000 rebels was planned, but local members of the republican party hesitated to cooperate with such allies and the plot failed.

In other cases, attempted cooperation between the republicans and the popular organizations took the form of mixed groups, which remained only loosely connected with the clandestine revolutionary movement. Their style of work resembled that of the traditional secret societies and their members felt more at their ease than they would in the modern republican groups. These bands of 'para-republicans' preserved the names, titles and ceremonies borrowed from the familiar tradition of the Elder Brother Society and the Triads; their chiefs were called 'Grand Dragons', and the grades were copied from those in use in the Ming dynasty. They also practised initiation rites. One group of this kind was the Society of the Dragon Flower (*Lung-hua Hui*), founded in 1904 by the republicans of Chekiang. Another was the League of Common Relief (*T'ung-chi Kung*), set up in Kweichow in 1905 by members of the Triad working with the T'ung-men Hui.

However, these efforts to create a 'united front', which would coordinate peasant rebelliousness with the modern revolutionary movement, produced no very startling results. The republicans were often suspicious of the secret societies as 'unreliable, unpredictable and undependable'. The reaction of the republican militants of the north-east, who refused to cooperate with the Red Beards, is typical. Anti-Manchu sentiment undoubtedly provided something resembling a common ideology for the republicans and the Triads; but it was a far cry from the dream of Ming restoration to the image of a republican China modelled on the United States, to which many republican leaders looked, including Sun Yat-sen himself. In the last analysis, the class consciousness of many republicans, linked as they were to a modern bourgeoisie which had scarcely freed itself from landlordism, or was even more directly connected to the gentry, hardly encouraged them to give any support to the struggle of the poor peasantry. The latter played an important role in the political and military struggles of the autumn of 1911 which succeeded in overthrowing both the Manchu dynasty and the imperial system.

On the surface, however, the revolution of 1911 seems to have owed little to mass action. It was in the towns – Wu-ch'ang, Nanking, Chungking and Shanghai – that the revolutionary offen-

25 Sun Yat-sen (fifth from the left in the front row) with members of the first cabinet of republican China, Nanking, January 1912.

sives occurred which led to the proclamation of the republic on 10 October. The political initiative had been taken by militants among the modern republicans, members of the T'ung-meng Hui, officers of the New Army and members of the commercial bourgeoisie. The form which the new regime took, a representative republic with a parliament and cabinet, showed that the republicans were familiar with the political systems of the West; it had little to do with the traditional ideology of peasant rebellions. It is in this sense that the revolution of 1911 was a revolution of a new type, and not a 'change of Mandate' in the traditional sense. Yet it is no coincidence that the Chinese term for revolution in the modern sense is the old word *ke-ming*, meaning 'removal of the Mandate'. In fact, the republican activities in the towns would not have succeeded if these towns had not in many cases been surrounded by 'old-style' popular forces – the armed members of secret societies. The action of the peasants, in moving on the towns in this way, was not so different, as it might at first seem, from the attack of the armed rebels of Li Tzu-ch'eng on Peking in 1644, which brought the Ming dynasty to an end.

In Szechuan, to take one example, the T'ung-meng Hui would not have been capable of occupying the provincial capital and the towns in the northern part of the province without the assistance of the peasant forces of the Elder Brother Society and other similar groups, such as the Society of Filial Piety and Righteousness (*Hsiao-i Hui*). Landless peasants were also very numerous in the Army of Comrades (*T'ung-chih Chün*), organized by the T'ung-meng Hui and the Elder Brother Society in order to attack the Manchu garrisons.

In Kwangtung the contribution of the peasants was even more marked. The T'ung-meng Hui had established contact with armed units, the *min-chün* (people's armies), which had appeared spontaneously some time earlier. These peasant bandits – poor peasants, agricultural labourers, rural artisans and outlaws (*lü-lin*) – were inspired by a kind of primitive populism; the term *min* in the philosophy of Mencius implied the concept of a historical force capable of resisting despotism. More than 100,000 *min-chün* joined Ch'en Chiung-ming, the military leader of the T'ung-meng Hui, surrounded Canton and entered it in November 1911.

In the north-west, on 17 November, a thousand peasants affiliated to the Triads attacked the town of Ning-hsia, opened the prisons and proclaimed independence from Peking – actions typical of peasant rebels throughout Chinese history. The great city of Sian, seat of the governor-general of the north-west, was also occupied on 22 October by peasant troops of the Elder Brother Society, the leaders of which had taken the decision to launch an offensive as soon as the news of the success of the republicans at Wu-ch'ang had arrived – the local members of the T'ung-meng Hui having failed to do so.

In other regions, however, the republicans were not able, or perhaps did not try, to coordinate their actions with the perpetual manifestations of agrarian unrest. In Honan, where the republicans did not manage to take power and where the conservatives remained masters of the situation, a powerful peasant revolt of a purely traditional kind had broken out just at the time when the revolutionaries were triumphing in central China. Thousands of peasants, under the leadership of the Green Gang (*Ch'ing-pang*), rose against excessive taxation and inscribed on their banners the traditional slogan, 'Kill the rich and help the poor!'

This new wave of peasant unrest was an integral part of the republican revolution of 1911, though it was unjustly overshadowed by the success of the republican movement in the cities. Sometimes the new organs of state, in which the radicals had been rapidly supplanted by the gentry, who showed a remarkable aptitude for jumping on the revolutionary bandwagon, themselves undertook the repression of their former allies. Such was the case in Szechuan and Hunan, where the new provincial governments ruthlessly turned on the secret societies. In the north-west, on the other hand, the wave of peasant unrest continued for several years, in what have been erroneously called the 'White Wolf Riots', under the leadership of a peasant called Pai Lang (which can mean 'white wolf' in Chinese). These peasants persisted until 1914 in their revolt against the new President of the Republic, Yuan Shih-k'ai, and other conservatives who had taken over the revolution for their own profit. The ideology of Pai Lang's bands was strongly marked by peasant radicalism and primitive populism. They called for the overthrow of Yuan Shih-k'ai and the establishment of 'good government'; they occupied large parts of the provinces of Shansi, Shensi and Kansu, and were suppressed only after the Peking government had launched several military expeditions against them.

It is precisely by giving due emphasis to the contribution of the peasantry to the process of revolution in 1911 that we can arrive at a balanced assessment of it. The revolution may have radically transformed the very form of government and replaced the ancient empire with a republican system – rare in the world at that time, outside the Americas; but it did nothing to change the structure of social relations, particularly in the rural areas. The peasants, who had contributed so actively to the fall of the empire, remained at the mercy of the landlords and the agents of the state, even if the latter now appeared under new names. This set-back for the peasants led them, after a period of uncertainty and return to old forms of struggle, to search for new perspectives. The frustration provoked by the almost artificial nature of the revolution of 1911 was one of the factors which led to the explosion of agrarian struggles between 1925 and 1950.

4 The Pattern of Peasant Unrest in Early Modern China

Peasant movements continued throughout the whole period between the Opium Wars and the fall of the Manchu dynasty, for longer perhaps than at any other time in the history of imperial China. Not one of the eighteen provinces was untouched; millions of peasants rose in revolt, under the banner of either the Boxers or the Triads, wreaking vengeance on brutal officials or burning government offices, or, in the case of the Taipings, attempting to realize an ambitious utopian dream.

From 1840 to 1911 the peasant struggle was never abandoned, though its vigour was far from constant. It reached a climax in the decade after 1850 and then slowed down. At the end of the century another crisis occurred under the influence, this time, of foreign pressure, and contributed, as we have seen, to the fall of the dynasty. This rhythm reflected the complex evolution of the Chinese political situation, which no longer involved only the confrontation between popular forces and the imperial regime, but was now complicated by the effects of imperialism and foreign interests. In the region of Canton at the time of the First Opium War, peasant wisdom had given expression to the new situation in the well-known saying, 'The people are afraid of the officials, the officials fear the foreign devils, but the foreign devils fear the people.' The new balance of forces offered new opportunities to the peasant movement and at the same time brought it into conflict with a new enemy. It is no coincidence that the two great waves of peasant activity, from 1850 to 1870 and from 1895 to 1911, corresponded to the main thrusts of imperialist pressure upon China. The intervening period was one of relative stability, in which China and the Western powers arrived at a temporary *modus vivendi* on the basis of the treaties and the politics of 'limited westernization'.

If the peasant movement of this period was fundamentally linked with the general political situation of China, it was certainly influenced as well by other factors which are less well understood. Agricultural disasters undoubtedly played an important role. The floods of 1853, when the Yellow River abruptly changed course and flowed into the sea 500 miles from its previous estuary, contributed to the distress of the peasants of north China which led to the Nien rebellion. The famines of 1896–98 preceded the Boxer uprising. Much less is known, however, about the changes in the agrarian economy of the country, about the evolution of land rents, agricultural prices and the rural labour market, about the decline of village handicraft industries upon which peasant families traditionally depended and with which modern industry was already in competition. The explosion of peasant unrest between 1850 and 1870 was undoubtedly the result of an agrarian crisis which had been developing since the beginning of the century. In the period of relative political stability, called by official historians the 'T'ung Chih Restoration', there was a temporary amelioration of agrarian relations. This was the result of the demographic bloodletting which suppression of the rebellions had involved, of internal migrations, both of which eased the pressure on the land, and of the tightened control of the gentry, who had emerged triumphant from the conflict. But a new crisis of the rural economy, the precise causes of which are no better understood, seems to have developed around the end of the nineteenth century and led directly to the countless peasant riots in the years 1909 to 1911.

The peasant movements of the end of the Ch'ing period clearly had the same characteristics as those of previous periods, the same narrowness of base, the same primitive forms of struggle, the same archaic kinds of ideology. The forms of alliance between peasants and other social groups were no different, and there was still no clear distinction between insurgency and banditry. Certain peasant movements, to be sure, were marginally influenced by the West – the religion of the Taipings, for example, or the Boxers' reaction to imperialism – but the permanent characteristics of peasant unrest were clearly predominant.

The most important of these was probably the narrowly regional nature of peasant insurrection. None of the great movements of the Chinese peasantry after 1840 succeeded in spreading beyond fairly limited geographical boundaries. Each secret society had its own strictly delineated zone of influence, from which it was incapable of emerging and beyond which it did not even attempt to mobilize the peasants. The Hung-hu-tzu were confined to the north-east of China, the Black Flags to the south-west; the Elder Brother Society had no influence outside the Yangtze valley, nor did the Boxers appear in south China. The Nien failed once their ambitions led them to campaign outside their home territory – the sandy zone between the Hwai and Yellow Rivers – and launch expeditions to the east and west. The failure of the Taiping attack on Peking and of their final desperate campaign in the north-west show the regional nature of the rebellion, its inability to expand into areas where the particular political and social conditions which had given it birth did not exist.

These peasant movements were not only localized in the country as a whole, but also tended to confine themselves to parts of provinces. The traditional seed-bed of peasant insurrection was not in the middle of a province, where the rice-growing plains were thickly populated and economically well developed, but along the wooded, mountainous borders between provinces. Such areas were less accessible to the forces of repression. Since government control over these inter-provincial frontiers was attenuated, they constituted a kind of administrative no-man's-land. Even if the provincial bureaucratic machine as such was well organized, rebels had little fear that the authorities of several provinces, often jealous of each other and incapable of coordinating their efforts, could mount a combined operation against them.

This localization within the border regions of several provinces is characteristic of the Nien movement and shows its close resemblance to the ancient model. The activities of the early Taipings, too, in the period when they called themselves the God-worshippers, were limited to a few mountainous districts between Kwangtung and Kwangsi. The Hung-hu-tzu and Black Flags were also typically regional, though both were active along national rather than inter-provincial boundaries – the Hung-hu-tzu between China and Russian Siberia, and the Black Flags on the frontier with Vietnam. The P'ing-liu-li revolt of 1906, the only military operation of the republicans which, thanks to the Triads, succeeded in gaining mass peasant support, took place in the isolated regions between Hunan and Kiangsi. In all these movements one can discern a kind of geopolitical 'law' of peasant rebellion in China – a pattern which the Chinese Communists discovered in their turn and used in the struggle against the Kuomintang and the Japanese.

From this point of view, the participation of peasants in the revolution of 1911 underlines the transitional character of the period. For the first time, peasant movements broke out simultaneously from one end of the country to the other; for now they were linked with a new, nationwide political force – the republican movement. But peasant participation, and indeed that of the rural gentry, whose political horizons were similarly limited, was still of an essentially local character and was not equally active everywhere. Consequently there was uneven development of the republican movement from province to province.

The localized character of the peasant movements was itself the reflection of the fragmented nature of peasant economy, which had as yet been only superficially influenced by the penetration of capitalism into the rural areas. As in past centuries, the political world of the peasant did not extend beyond the areas in which the goods which he himself produced or consumed were apt to circulate.

Nor had there been any fundamental evolution in the peasants' methods of struggle or in their ideology. Primitive violence still predominated and struck against the whole machinery of oppression and exploitation which weighed upon them – the *yamen*, the houses of the rich, prisons, officials, tax collectors, usurers, convoys of merchants, loan receipts and tax registers. It was still struggle by force alone, which could be limited to individual brutality, but might, on the other hand, lead to the formation of immense armies like those of the Taipings. But the peasants had no arms other than those they could find in the countryside, spears, clubs and knives; hence the names of several peasant secret societies, such as the Great

26–29 Membership tokens struck by the Chin Ch'ien society, part of the Triad system of secret societies.

Knives (*Ta-tao Hui*) or Red Spears (*Hung-ch'iang Hui*). Only occasionally they had old guns. As to peasant ideology, apart from the Christian borrowings of the Taipings and the anti-Western proclamations of the Boxers, it remained the same as it had been before the nineteenth century. The peasants still dreamed of an idealized past, perhaps of the Ming dynasty or, in the case of the Taipings, of even more archaic institutions. They were vigorously egalitarian, as is shown by the Land Law of the Taipings and the division of spoils among the Nien and the Hung-hu-tzu. They exalted the virtues of rebellion; they were feminist; they made no distinction between the earthly struggle against the established order and religious revelation, between the superstitious conviction that they merited salvation and the power to transcend the laws of nature through the practice of esoteric rites.

The rebellious peasantry of the period between 1840 and 1911 continued to enjoy appreciable support from other sections of society. Their most important allies were also from the world of the countryside, but were free from the servitude of agricultural production – porters, stevedores, boatmen, pedlars, rural artisans (often itinerant) and charcoal burners. There were also various *éléments déclassés*, victims of the political, economic and military crisis : ruined peasants, vagabonds, disbanded soldiers, wandering labourers, smugglers, mendicant monks, beggars and brigands. This picturesque and picaresque underworld played a great part in the struggles of the Chinese peasantry. They enjoyed a mobility which the day-to-day work in the fields and the inexorable demands of the seasons denied to the peasants ; they travelled far and carried news, rebellious slogans or forbidden writings ; their mental horizon was wider and their critique of society more radical, and their participation in peasant revolts helped to make them less localized. The Elder Brother Society, whose sphere of activity was most extensive, in fact spread in a region of China where long-distance communication was easiest – that of the navigable Yangtze and its network of tributaries. It was, moreover, among the itinerant elements of society that peasant rebellions found their leaders. Among the Taiping *wangs* there was a charcoal burner, another was a porter reduced to unemployment by the shift of the commercial routes towards the east after 1842. The chief leader of the Nien, as we have said, was a salt-smuggler. The two main leaders of the Boxers were a disbanded soldier and a boatman from the Grand Canal, ruined by the development of steam navigation. The founder of the Black Flags, Liu Yung-fu, was the son of a poor peasant whose social status continually declined as he moved from one district to another in search of work. Once his last parcel of land was sold, Li's father eked out a living as a butcher's assistant or a wine distiller. Left alone in the world at the age of 17, Liu Yung-fu lived by collecting mushrooms ; he worked as a boatman and a poacher, selling his fish or his mushrooms and sleeping in stables. Such was the man who became a military commander feared by the imperial authorities of Vietnam, by proud Chinese governors and by the French generals of the Third Republic.

In addition to the rural artisans and the *éléments déclassés*, the peasants could also sometimes find allies among dissident members of the privileged classes, from the commercial class, and among the non-conformist gentry. Some merchants, indeed, sought to enrich themselves more rapidly, though more dangerously, through traffic with the secret societies, particularly in salt-smuggling, or in arms, opium, drugs, etc. Certain educated men of independent character refused the toadying and compromises implied by a normal career, the Confucian grades and the functions of an official; there were others who failed to pass the examinations and retired to their villages. The Taiping leader, Hung Hsiu-ch'üan, and one of his principal lieutenants, Shih Ta-k'ai, were men of this kind, and there were others among the Nien leadership.

Members of other sections of society who participated in peasant movements did so, however, more because of individual rebelliousness than because the strata which they came from were in economic or political opposition to the established order. Vagabonds and *éléments déclassés*, smugglers and dissident literati, broke only as individuals with 'respectable' society, because of bad luck, or ambitions, or because of their strength of character, and not on account of a common economic situation. As individuals they could help the peasant movements, but they could do nothing to overcome the limitations of these movements. The pre-proletariat, consisting of rural artisans, carriers, charcoal burners, miners and so on, represented a more coherent social force with its own economic objectives. But numerically they were weak; they were scattered and still too closely tied to the ancient rural economy to be able to bring to the peasants what they lacked.

The fact that until 1911 peasant movements were unable to establish solid links with the modern currents in Chinese society shows how close they remained to the peasant revolts of the past. From this point of view it is significant that the Taipings' turn towards the West – their interest in modernization, their search for a synthesis between Christianity and the traditional ideology of the peasants – should have come to nothing. This unprecedented attempt terminated with the fall of Nanking in 1864 and left no trace behind, and the popular movements which followed remained completely indifferent to its modern and Western innovations. Relations between the peasant movement and the radical republicans were superficial; they were hardly more than tangential contacts between two political currents which attack the same enemy, but whose social bases and historical perspectives are completely different, if not incompatible, and who inhabit two different worlds.

After 1840 the peasant movement remained relatively autonomous with respect to the general historical conditions in which it existed. Although China was being brought under the control of the Western powers, although the grip of the unequal treaties tightened and the fate of the Chinese government came increasingly to depend upon the general policies of the powers, there was fundamentally no change in the objectives, in the rhythm and structure, or in the ideological character of the Chinese peasant movement. Even when the peasants became conscious of a new problem – that of the foreign domination of China – and reacted violently against it, they did so within the traditional framework provided by one of the most archaic secret societies, the I-ho Ch'üan, which had links with the even more venerable White Lotus, traceable to the twelfth century. The political and economic situation of the Chinese countryside had not been sufficiently or profoundly modified by Western penetration to allow the peasants to develop new historical perspectives. The new social forces in the towns, on the other hand, were too distant from the peasantry to be able to make the kind of contact with them which was to be the decisive factor in the twentieth century, when the Communists proved capable of mobilizing the rural masses. The political horizons of the republican revolutionaries and the modern reformers were completely different from those of the peasants, but basically just as narrow since they were limited to the 'modern' towns – the Treaty Ports. Even those republicans and reformers who did not come from landlord and gentry families, whose privileges stemmed from the exploitation of the peasantry, despised the latter as backward because they themselves were imbued with the idea of progress and thought that imitation of the Western model was all that mattered. They were incapable of taking in hand the real

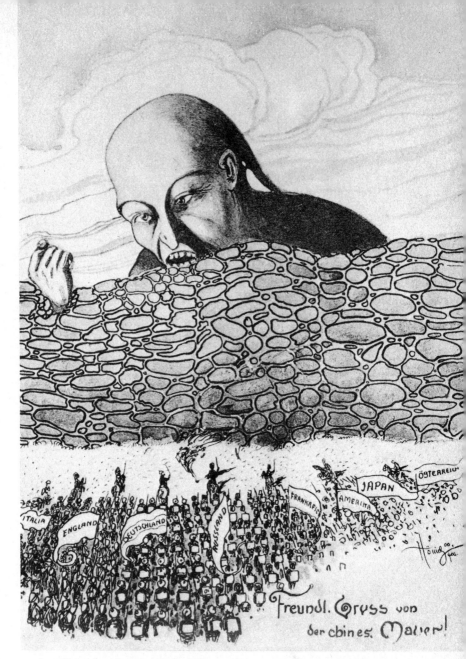

30 *Best Wishes from the Great Wall of China*, a characteristically prejudiced Western view (in this case German) of the Chinese situation: Italian, English, German, Russian, French, American, Japanese and Austrian troops prepare to invade.

problems of the peasantry or of mobilizing them for the achievement of a modern ideal of progress.

This does not mean, of course, that the repeated assaults of the peasants on the established order, the privileged classes and the state apparatus, from the Taiping rebellion to the revolution of 1911, had been entirely in vain. The struggle of the peasantry during this period had a real effect upon the fate of China; the constant threat of revolt maintained that permanent atmosphere of political insecurity which had characterized the imperial regime for centuries, symbolized by the battlemented walls of the towns – the architectural expression of social conflict, which might be more or less acute, but was always there. The potential strength of the peasant masses also explains the facility with which the aggressive Western powers had imposed their will upon China throughout the nineteenth century. Never, during the Opium Wars, the Sino-French War (1884–85), the Sino-Japanese War (1894–95), nor in 1900 with the siege of Peking, had the Western powers reduced China to a desperate military situation. Operations were localized and short-term. The imperial Chinese government surrendered so quickly on these occasions and gave away financial, territorial and political privileges because it feared the instability of the hinterland, the countryside. The government dared not launch protracted, widespread popular resistance such as the Japanese invaders were to experience between 1937 and 1945. They dared not arm and mobilize the people against an external enemy lest they turn on their own masters, as was to happen to the Kuomintang and the landlords after 1946. From this point of view, the peasant movement after the Opium Wars contributed as much to the fall of the dynasty by the ever-present threat which it posed, as by the revival of its activities between 1900 and 1911 and by the mass rising in the autumn of that year.

It is certain, too, that the credit for checking Western plans for the partition of China, so popular in certain business circles, and even in some Western chancelleries at the end of the nineteenth century, must go to the peasant movement. The Boxer incident put an immediate end to such hopes. Though derided as 'backward', 'xenophobic' and 'superstitious', this outburst nevertheless caused considerable fear. At a time when the rivalry among the powers was becoming more and more acute, it made them renounce their intended dismemberment of what they disdainfully called 'the sick man of the Far East'.

But it would be wrong to overemphasize the positive contribution of the peasant movements to the history of China. They may have added to the difficulties of the imperial regime, they may have obstructed the designs of the West and hastened the fall of the dynasty; but they were never capable of putting China on to a new historical path, more favourable to their own interests. They did not, nor were they able to, produce a revolutionary programme or a revolutionary solution.

The climax of their activities was to enter the towns in a spectacular act of revenge against the privileged classes. The 'Asiatic' town was not like that of medieval Europe, where a new social and economic force, that of bourgeois capitalism, grew up. In societies dominated by the contradiction between the rural communities and the despotic state, the town was the nerve centre of the administrative apparatus (the *yamen*) and the residence of members of the ruling class, the scholar-officials. The towns were also centres of those economic activities essential to the political and social definition of the term: reservoirs of urban labour where luxury goods were produced and where rural products for the support of urban populations were collected and distributed. In the final analysis, however, the towns were politically passive, pawns in the struggle between the state and the peasants. When the peasant struggle developed to a certain stage, when sufficient forces were mobilized, it could culminate in the invasion of a town or city by the rebels, as when the Taipings occupied Nanking, An-ch'ing, Soochow, Hangchow and several other political and commercial centres in the lower Yangtze valley, or when the Red Turbans and mountain outlaws took Fatshan and Shunte near Canton. In the same way, in October and November 1911, peasants mobilized by the secret societies contributed to the overthrow of the dynasty by occupying certain large towns. This is the historical background to the momentous world strategy which Lin Piao put forward in September 1965 – that the people of the area of 'revolutionary storms', of the 'rural areas of the world', that is, the people of Asia, Africa and Latin America, should surround the 'cities of the world' – the industrial countries (including, by implication, the USSR). This strategy developed from the historical experience of the Chinese Communists and the policies which had brought them to power in 1949, after the fall of the great Kuomintang-controlled cities to peasant guerillas. But at the same time the strategy had a more ancient heritage, and continued a pattern which had always been present in the struggles of Chinese peasants in the pre-industrial era.

Once in the cities what could rebellious peasantry do there? They could only withdraw, as in 1911, or pillage and be finally wiped out, as at Fatshan and Shunte in 1854; or they might try to establish a rebel order which could never be anything more than a replica of the traditional regime. The Taipings created what was in effect a new imperial system, based upon the total power of the ruler and his court. Their regime could only survive by instituting a demanding fiscal system for the support of its armies and of its leaders; the new 'feudal' order of *wangs* lived at the expense of their faithful followers and subjects. If peasant revolts were not incapacitated by the exigencies of a new kind of establishment, they remained at the mercy of another peril – that of degeneration into simple banditry. This applies to the Black Flags, the Hung-hu-tzu and, to a certain extent, to the Nien. But in either case peasant rebellions failed to give sustained stimulation and encouragement to the social movements out of which they had risen. Whether peasant insurrection found expression in the establishment of a rebel state, with all the constraints this implied, as in the case of the Taipings, or took the form of bands of outlaws gradually hunted down by the authorities, like the Nien, these peasant rebellions, in the end, could only survive at the expense of the villages, from which the rebels became increasingly isolated and which they eventually alienated. The struggles between insurgents and the authorities, in so far as they were prolonged, took place above the level of the villages, so to speak, which were themselves, to a certain extent, in the position of a 'third force'. The villages had their own rural militia, which often began by supporting a revolt, because of the exactions of the state and the privileged classes, as in the case of the Red Turbans in 1854 and the Nien. But the villages were soon disappointed in their association with the rebels, who could never escape from their dilemma – the choice between 'neo-feudalism' and banditry. Thus the officials could gradually re-establish their authority in the countryside, by means of the local gentry.

None of these revolts and rebellions, in spite of their vigour, proved capable of destroying the traditional fabric of Chinese rural society, of breaking the innumerable and sometimes invisible threads by which, for centuries, the gentry had maintained their hold over the peasantry; not merely by rents and corvée services, but also by their works of charity, their intellectual prestige, by arbitration in private disputes, administration of public works and the granaries, and by their role as intermediaries with officialdom. The countless peasant insurrections, in spite of the huge numbers they mobilized, remained within the traditional Chinese system, within the ancient mode of production, and were incapable of breaking free from it whatever allies they found among the *éléments déclassés* and non-agricultural rural trades.

The peasant rebellions of the nineteenth century cannot, therefore, be said to constitute a peasant revolution in the sense of a historical process which tends to bring radical change. For that, China had to await the twentieth century.

5   Peasants and the Revolution of 1924–27

From the time of the republican revolution to the War of Resistance against Japan, the condition of the peasants of China steadily deteriorated. The landowners, many of whom now lived in the towns, had new, 'modern' needs; but their revenue came from the same source as before and had the same 'feudal' character; they had no choice but to demand always more and more from the peasants. Rents augmented and were increasingly exacted in terms of currency. In the region of Nan-t'ung (Kiangsu), average rents rose from 1·31 *yuan* per *mou* (one-sixth of an acre) in 1905 to 4·14 *yuan* in 1924. In addition there might be 'rent deposits', again a money payment, which could amount to double the annual rent. Such deposits were increasingly insisted upon, and the tenants who did not meet their obligations lost their deposits. Even independent peasants were tied to the landlords by usury. In four districts of Chekiang in 1930, between 49 per cent and 59 per cent of peasants were in debt. Concentration of property in the hands of landlords proceeded inexorably, by the seizure of the land of ruined peasants. Near Wu-hsi in 1929, poor peasants, composing 69 per cent of the population, owned less than 14 per cent of the land, while landlords – 6 per cent of the population – owned 47 per cent.

Apart from the increasing burdens upon them resulting from their position of social dependence, the peasants also suffered from the effects of the political crisis and the general economic disruption which accompanied it. After 1911, and particularly after the death, in 1916, of Yuan Shih-k'ai, the last forceful figure of the *Ancien Régime*, China was the victim of rival military cliques and their incessant wars. For the peasants this meant endless requisitions and corvée, insecurity and pillage. Between 1916 and 1924 the average number of provinces ravaged each year by civil war was seven; between 1925 and 1930 it was fourteen. For the peasants there was little difference between the troops of contesting warlords and the bands of brigands that infested the countryside. Bandits were often no more than badly paid soldiers or deserters, and many soldiers behaved like bandits, so the organization of village self-defence against the depredations of soldiers and bandits was one of the essential elements of the peasant movement in 1920–30. Another enemy was the tax-collector, whether he was sent by the central government (when this was possible) or by the provincial authorities or the various military cliques who controlled them. The most frequent abuses were surtaxes, which were imposed at the slightest pretext, and taxes collected in advance. In Szechuan in 1933 taxes were already collected for 1971; in another district a sum eleven times the annual tax was collected between October 1931 and March 1933.

The distress of the peasantry was greatly worsened by economic disruption resulting from the anarchic penetration of capitalism, the absence of any overall economic policy, the decline of central power, and the civil war. The exchange rate between copper and silver continued to rise: in one region of central China from 2,300 copper coins to 1 silver *yuan* in 1922 to 15,600 in 1931. This brought a decrease in the revenue of peasants (mostly in copper cash) and an increase in taxes and rents, which were calculated in silver. Equally serious was the decline of rural handicraft industry. To make ends meet, peasant families traditionally depended upon subsidiary production for the slack season, or carried on by the women and children: weaving, basket-making, brick-making, brewing, etc. These home industries now had to compete with imported goods, with the products of cities like Shanghai, and with goods such as Japanese silk and Indian tea, which sold better on the international market. The undermining of local industry was only partly compensated for by the increased employment of village labour, in spinning or the production of matches, for example, by merchants in the towns. The general decline of village handicrafts helped to bring the agrarian crisis to a head.

Natural calamities, the constant scourge of the countryside, were more critical now that the state machinery was in ruins and the local authorities were incapable of meeting emergencies. The great famine of 1920–21 in north China took a toll of hundreds of thousands, and that of Honan, in 1941, of millions. Several terrible floods devastated vast regions near the Hwai and Yangtze Rivers in the early 'thirties.

Flight from the villages gave little relief. Millions of peasants migrated to the new lands of Manchuria, to the South Seas – the colonies of the Western powers in South-east Asia and the Pacific, Malaya, Vietnam, Indonesia, the Philippines and Hawaii; they flooded into the cities as well. Urban industry developed rapidly in this period, and the railways, ports and mines also drew upon peasant labour. But in spite of the extent of these movements of population, they affected only a minute fraction of the total peasantry and were limited to certain regions. Manchuria was above all settled by peasants from Shantung and Hopei; the workers of Shanghai came mostly from the neighbouring districts of Kiangsu, and Chinese emigrants overseas were nearly all from Kwangtung and Fukien. The great majority of the peasants remained in their villages with their misery.

Between the two World Wars the traditional polarization of society between two antagonistic forces – landlords and poor peasants – became much more acute. Capitalist development of the agricultural economy was obstructed by the situation in the country as a whole, by China's dependence on foreign economic interests, by conservatism, by the restricted nature of the market and by technological stagnation. Even where commercialized agriculture developed to supply food and raw materials for the industrial centres, it did so within the framework of 'feudal' landlord economy, and not as capitalist (*kulak*) agriculture. The peasantry became increasingly impoverished within the traditional system of social dependence, while the power of the landlords grew.

It was not merely the economic power of the landlords, their system of exploitation, which grew, but their political power as well, due to the decay of public authority and the disorganization of the whole administrative structure through governmental crises

31 Victims of famine, July 1930.

and civil war. Hitherto the landlords had been the mainstay of political stability, experienced, well organized, capable of controlling the peasantry and of providing the authorities with a relatively solid social base. Neither the warlords, the Kuomintang, nor the Japanese in the areas which they were to occupy, could dispense with their services. They often lived in the towns now, but it was from among their relatives and protégés that those who oppressed and lived off the peasantry were recruited: the bailiffs and stewards who not only collected the rents and debts due to their masters, but also took a substantial cut for their own benefit; the tax-gatherers in whose registers the landlords' holdings were on an authorized 'special list', allowing them to pay taxes in inverse proportion to their wealth, or not at all; the police chiefs and their men, increasingly numerous under the Kuomintang after 1927, as political control tightened and penetrated into the villages; the labour-contractors, who came to the countryside to buy women and children as virtual slaves for the factories in the cities. The landlords were now so powerful that they could not only depend upon this whole army of auxiliaries and upstarts, but often had their own private armies (*min-t'uan*) as well.

By the abolition of the Confucian examination system in 1905 and of the degrees which went with it, the gentry had lost the traditional symbol of their power, but not the power itself. By moving to the towns they had put an end to the long-standing ambiguity which had resulted from their Confucian status. Until the nineteenth century the rural gentry (*shen-shih*) were masters of the land (*ti-chu*), masters of learning (by the achievement of Confucian degrees) and masters of political power. This involved a strict system of exploitation and control, as well as the equivocal functions of charity, mediation and arbitration. A member of the gentry was able to intervene on behalf of a peasant with the local official; he also engaged in matters of public concern – the administration of granaries, schools, charitable foundations and public works. This equivocal situation had now come to an end. The landlord no longer lived in the countryside and had, in any case, ceased to fulfil any official function. For the peasants he was henceforth an enemy and nothing more. So the confrontation between peasant and landlord was more radical, more brutal in the twentieth century than it had been in the nineteenth. The Confucian rationalizations had gone, giving way to the hatred which found expression in the mass trials of landlords after Land Reform in 1947, and which is reflected in the films, peasant novels and plays of the Yenan period.

The profound disruption of the Chinese countryside and the whole of Chinese society in the twentieth century had another important consequence: the proliferation of rural *éléments déclassés* – ruined peasants, vagabonds, unemployed labourers, outlaws, pedlars and so on. There had always been many – now they could be counted in tens of millions. They were at the service of the peasant revolution, but could also be recruited by the forces of suppression, the armies of

32 Kuomintang hostility towards the Communists grew in 1927, culminating in Chiang Kai-shek's *coup* in Shanghai on 12 April against his former allies on the Northern Expedition: shown here is an execution squad on the march.

the warlords, the troops of the Kuomintang and the puppets of the Japanese.

Thus the social prerequisites for a real revolution matured in the Chinese countryside in the twentieth century. Often, however, peasant unrest continued to find expression in ancient forms, in the activities of the secret societies, spontaneous riots and rural banditry. It is probable indeed that these archaic forms of struggle were capable of mobilizing greater numbers of peasants than their modern counterparts, such as the peasant associations of 1925–27, the peasant soviets in the years between 1928 and 1935, and the anti-Japanese guerilla bases after 1937. Nevertheless, it was these modern organizations that accomplished the agrarian revolution, which the secret societies and the bandits remained just as incapable of achieving as they had always proved.

The most typical of these archaic forms was the riot, often provoked by fiscal exactions. In June 1933 the peasants of five districts in western Szechuan formed an army to resist taxes (*k'ang-shui-chün*). In other cases rioters even ventured to attack armies, as in 1931 in northern Fukien, when tens of thousands of peasants attacked troops whose exactions had become intolerable. At Soochow in 1931 rent collectors were the object of the fury of desperate peasants, who destroyed their houses and clashed with the police. For the period 1922–31 alone, a historian has noted 197 incidents involving farmers or landlords, reported in two Shanghai newspapers. Thirty-three per cent of these incidents were violent and sometimes involved bloodshed. The list was clearly far from complete.

Other incidents were provoked by authoritarian measures of 'modernization' imposed on the peasants by Kuomintang officials after 1927. Though technically justifiable, these measures conflicted with peasant customs. Because of the system of feudal subordination, an increase in agricultural production was more likely to benefit the landlords than the peasants themselves. Any action of the authorities, at whose hands the peasants had always suffered exactions of one kind or another, was automatically suspect. This explains why some peasants in Hopei attacked 2,800 workers from Shantung, who had come to build a road which would be used for the transport of goods in times of difficulty and avoid such disasters as the famine of 1920–21. In the north of Chekiang province, 10,000 peasants revolted because they had been forced to buy silkworm eggs specially selected by government experts; they killed an official and burned the office of the rural reconstruction service. Yet this was at a time when Japanese silk, of a superior quality, was competing effectively with Chinese silk on the world market.

Many of these riots were spontaneous, but they were often connected with, if not stirred up by, the secret societies – still a potent influence, though no less scattered and localized than they had always been. In the province of Szechuan in 1920–21, the emotive names of the Taipings and Boxers reappeared; rebellious peasants, supported by Taoist priests, used potions which were said to give invulnerability and wore Ming-style clothes. The Red Spear movement, around 1925–30, was concentrated in the northern provinces of Shantung, Honan, Shensi and Shansi. It originated in peasant self-defence, in the squads which were spontaneously formed in the villages to protect them against the depredations of bandits, the exactions of fiscal officials and the looting of soldiers – so common at the height of the warlord period. The Red Spears had no central leadership, but the various local commanders joined together in a vague federation. They used secret rites of initiation, amulets of invulnerability and observed certain religious prohibitions. From a political point of view their movement represented the desire of the peasants for peace and order, as shown by the frequent use of the term 'good sovereign', their protests against the misery of the time and the abuses of the regime rather than against the regime itself. The Red Spears fought against bandits and looters, but not against landlords; the movement nevertheless mobilized hundreds of thousands of villagers in north China, and was of sufficient consequence to lead the Communist Party and the left wing of the Kuomintang, during the revolution of 1925–27, to attempt to infiltrate its ranks, in an effort to lead the peasantry towards more modern methods of struggle. In general such attempts were in vain.

The secret societies continued to be very active in the early 'thirties; they continued to organize communal self-defence in the villages against the triple scourge – bandits, soldiers and tax-gatherers – which continued to devastate the countryside, even after the victory of the Kuomintang in 1927 and the formation of the 'National government' at Nanking. But their activity was always episodic and localized, as in the Great Knife Society (*Ta-tao Hui*) rising in 1929, on the border between the provinces of Kirin and Feng-t'ien in the north-east, provoked by banditry and tax-collectors. Not only did the secret societies not challenge the social system itself – only its injustices – but their limited horizons led to factionalism. In September 1928 in northern Kiangsu there was a bloody clash between the members of the Big Knife and the Little Knife Societies, the former consisting of local peasants and the latter of unwelcome newcomers from other regions who had come in search of land. Nevertheless, the influence which kept the secret societies alive – the support of the peasant masses – was so strong that in 1936, at the height of the Japanese threat, Mao Tse-tung went so far as to propose to the Elder Brother Society, the most influential of the secret societies, a political pact and united front against Japan.

> In the past, you supported the restoration of the Han and the extermination of the Manchus; today, we support resistance to Japan and the saving of the country. You support striking at the rich and helping the poor; we support striking at the local bullies and dividing up the land. You despise wealth and defend justice, and you gather together all the heroes and brave fellows in the world; we unite the exploited and oppressed peoples and groups of the whole world. Our views and positions are therefore quite close.

In fact, if the secret societies of the towns frequently collaborated with the Japanese, the societies which had the support of the peasants of north China participated in the struggle against the same enemy, often cooperating with the Communist guerillas (see Chapter 7).

There did not exist at this time a clear distinction between secret-society activity and banditry. As soon as there was a wave of popular discontent, their experience, their politico-religious armoury and their organizations put them in a position to provide leadership. When the wave of insurrection subsided, they went back to their rackets, to looting or smuggling. Banditry as such is a primitive form of peasant protest; it is a road of individual escape which allows ruined peasants and *éléments déclassés* to survive on the margins of society. The 1920s and '30s were the great years of Chinese banditry, reflecting the gravity of the rural crisis. In 1923 a bandit gang under a man called Yang Lao-jen even held up the luxurious 'Blue Express' which ran between Tientsin and Nanking, in the middle of the countryside, taking prisoner some thirty Westerners, including a member of the Rockefeller family.

The fact that this revival of banditry was both a by-product of the crisis of the peasantry and a consequence of the collapse of public authority is underlined by the account of an American Episcopalian missionary in 1925 of a meeting with bandits as he was walking by night in the town of Hsing-hua in Fukien:

'I was formerly a farmer,' said one, 'but I got involved with a group of men over water supply for the irrigation of our fields. One of the group being a police inspector of course had special influence with the government. Taking advantage of it, he had me seized and handed over to the yamen, making false representations about me. The judge listening to his words rendered a decision against me. I was thrown into prison. I got my freedom by paying the sum of 120 dollars. I rebelled at this unjust treatment and seeing the present opportunity of becoming a brigand and getting revenge I proceeded to join. I succeeded in my objective. One night I led a group of fellow brigands and captured my enemies. It cost the group over a thousand dollars to get their freedom. Now they have joined a rival group of bandits and we must be constantly on our guard against an attack. . . .' 'I likewise was a farmer,' said another. 'Alas there was a feud that divided my village into opposite clans. The other faction was stronger than my group. One of their leaders also belonged to a bandit group, bringing this added strength to their side. My group saw no other way than to have one of their members to join a rival bandit group. I was selected as the one to do this.'

While some ruined peasants 'took to the hills', many others sought to escape from their misery by enrolling in the warlords' armies, or by going to work in factories; this is why the two processes of militarization and industrialization were both involved with a certain peasant radicalism, though their historical roots were, of course, much more complex.

Militarism in China in the 'twenties and 'thirties, the constant inter-provincial fighting between regional cliques, stemmed from the decline of central power, the weakness of the republic which had been formally established in 1911 and the intrigues of the great powers, Japan, France and Britain, whose protégés the warlords were. Their troops were recruited from the poor peasantry and

33 With bayonets fixed, British sailors parade in Shanghai, spring 1927; increasing unrest at this time obliged foreign powers to strengthen their garrisons in the city.

preserved something of the primitive brutality of peasant rebels. In 1921 a regional army mutinied at I-ch'ang on the Yangtze because the troops had not been paid for a long time. They sacked the town, held merchants to ransom and opened the prison – behaved, in fact, just as typical peasant rebels did when they occupied a town.

The same primitive peasant characteristics are found in the early Chinese labour movement. For the most part the workers were peasants who had recently migrated to the towns and who found the industrial environment totally strange and hostile. When their discontent against the long hours, low wages and the tyranny of foremen and labour contractors exploded, they did not organize strike committees, elaborate detailed demands or conduct a disciplined strike movement; they flared up abruptly, broke machinery and demolished buildings in a primitive kind of 'labour rebellion', actions strongly marked by peasant spontaneity.

These primitive, marginal or degraded forms of the peasant movement continued to have considerable significance right up to the end of the Second World War, if not until the Liberation of 1949. But 1949 was the culmination of the modern revolution, and this was only possible because there had been an increasing unity between the struggle of the peasant masses and the strategy of the modern revolutionary forces. This fusion took place in three stages: the revolution of 1924–27, led by the breakaway nationalist government in Canton; the shift of the Communist effort to the countryside between 1927 and 1935 (the period of the Kiangsi soviet); and third, the formation of peasant guerilla bases under Communist leadership from 1937 onwards, to fight first the Japanese and later the Kuomintang.

The Communist Party, formed in 1921, had originally but weak links with the peasant movement. As to the Kuomintang, heir of the republican victory of 1911 though speedily deprived of power, this party was even more isolated from rural struggles than it had been in the first years of the century, when the republicans had been seeking alliances with the secret societies against the Manchus. The relationship between these two political parties and the peasant movement changed completely in 1924. The Kuomintang and the republican government at Canton, under the influence of Sun Yat-sen, decided to make an alliance with the Communists – approved and even hoped for by the Comintern in Moscow. Chinese Communists became members of the Kuomintang, but preserved their own independent organization. They gave their support to the republican government which, for its part, adopted the new policy of alliance with the Communists, cooperation with the USSR and support for the workers' and peasants' movements. The last point in this policy shows the influence of the Communists at Canton. In the area under the control of the southern government, labour unions and peasant associations were not only tolerated, but helped and encouraged.

The government subsidized, for example, a school for peasant cadres established at Canton in 1925 under the direction of Mao Tse-tung, as a member of the Kuomintang. Initially this political development affected only the region of Canton, but after July 1926, with the launching of the Northern Expedition, the nationalist armies were able to conquer the whole of central China as far as the Yangtze, and a vast new area was opened up for the development of new forms of peasant struggle, by means of the Peasant Associations. The revolution of 1924–27 was a phase of vigorous advance for the peasant movement, which gave new impetus to the whole modern revolutionary process in this period.

The spectacular progress of the Peasant Associations in Hunan in 1926–27 is well known, thanks to the investigation and report made by Mao Tse-tung in January 1927, which has become a classic. The Peasant Associations, which sprang up as the southern revolutionary army advanced, were essentially instruments of the political struggle against landlords, gentry and local authorities. They took over the administration of rural affairs, fined the most arrogant of the local bigwigs or forced them to make contributions; the worst of them were paraded and ridiculed, imprisoned, banished and sometimes executed. The small-time village tyrants who controlled the local administration, police and armed guards were overthrown; district officials, magistrates and policemen were excluded from public affairs and forced to flee or hide. Taxes were reduced and the most unpopular ones abolished altogether.

Real power passed into the hands of the Peasant Associations – the new form of organization of the whole peasantry, not just of a minority, as the secret societies had been. Their main social strength came from the poor peasants, but rich and middle peasants were not excluded. They had their own militia and abolished the private armed bands of the landlords. Millions of village volunteers were armed with spears, and many with rifles. The Associations had actual political control, dealing with quarrels, planning social and economic administration, stamping out banditry. Clan and religious authorities were overthrown. The despotic authority of husbands was undermined and clan elders no longer dared to exclude women from ritual

34 Two Kuomintang leaders, Chiang Kai-shek and Wang Ching-wei, in Canton, November 1925. Though still dependent upon Russian military support in 1925, within a few years the Kuomintang broke away from its Communist wing, and, after a prolonged civil war, set up an exile government in Taiwan in 1949; in 1940, Wang Ching-wei was appointed head of a puppet government in Japanese-controlled China.

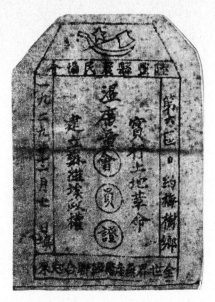

35, 36 Two Peasant Association membership cards of the second half of the 1920s; each displays a sun, badge of the Nationalists, and the hammer and sickle, thus symbolizing the Kuomintang-Communist alliance.

feasts. The wooden statues of village divinities were burned and fewer people consulted horoscopes or geomancers; the powerful movement had given the peasants self-confidence and helped to liberate them from their traditional fears.

The Peasant Associations also promulgated a number of social and moral, if not puritan, rules; they banned gambling, opium-smoking, the use of sedan-chairs by the rich, the distilling of alcohol, costly celebrations, obscene plays and begging. They sponsored peasant schools in place of the few existing state schools, with their artificially modernistic curricula, which had little real interest for the peasants.

The Associations did not undertake confiscation and distribution of land. Their leaders adhered to the joint programme of the Kuomintang and Communist Party, adopted in 1924, which called only for the limitation of rent and usury. They did not take direct radical measures, but nevertheless worked towards them; they resisted landlords' attempts to evict poor peasants, forbade speculation and the hoarding or exportation of rice from the province. They recommended the peasants to limit the number of pigs and fowl which they raised, in order to economize grain, and forbade the slaughter of animals. Attempts were made to set up cooperatives. The Associations also took over from the gentry even the most traditional of their functions – the administration of public works; they organized the repair of roads and dikes, either by making the landlords concerned undertake the work or else by means of labour brigades.

These were the 'fourteen great achievements' of the Hunan peasants, listed in the celebrated report by Mao Tse-tung; it was truly 'a great and unprecedented revolution in the countryside'. The Peasant Association movement arose in the context of the revolution of 1924–27, it profited from the advance of the southern armies but was, at the same time, limited and restricted by this fact; consequently there was no division or distribution of land. It was, nevertheless, a proof of the creative initiative of the peasants, and led to self-government in the spheres of administration, social and military organization and so on. In the final analysis this activity was based on the priority of politics over economics. It aimed, first of all, to break the political and moral domination of the ruling class, as a preliminary to the destruction of the feudal economic structure. It was a peasant revolution which left land reform for later. The Maoist slogan of the 1960s – 'politics in command' – fits it exactly.

The most spectacular upsurge of the Peasant Association movement during the revolution of 1924–27 took place in Hunan, but there were similar developments in Kiangsi and Chekiang. Near Canton, in the mountainous districts of Hai-feng and Lu-feng (Hailufeng), a peasant movement had started in 1922–23 under the leadership of the militant Communist, P'eng P'ai. Peasant Associations had been formed, which held their own against the armies of local militarists, overthrew the power of the gentry and imposed a 40 per cent reduction in land rents. Even in the north, in Honan, many Peasant Associations appeared in 1925–26, thanks to the relatively liberal attitude of the warlord Feng Yü-hsiang, but also because the activities of the Red Spears in the same region created a favourable atmosphere. In June 1926, Peasant Associations virtually existed only in Kwangtung and Honan, yet had a membership of approximately a million; by the end of January 1927, when Mao Tse-tung made his investigation, there were two million in Hunan alone. By June that year there was a total membership of some nine million, including $4\frac{1}{2}$ million in Hunan, and $2\frac{1}{2}$ million in Hupei, in the region of Wuhan where the nationalist government was then based.

What was the reason for this sudden upsurge of the peasant movement, the mobilization of so many millions of peasants? It was partly a result of the general political situation of the time. The destruction of the warlord regimes by the advance of the nationalist armies did not mean that the social base of these regimes, among the rural gentry and landlords, had been destroyed. The peasants knew this. Moderate though it was, the agrarian policy of the nationalist government was popular in the countryside. In 1925 and 1926 there were provincial congresses of the Peasant Associations in Kwangtung, and a national congress with delegates from all nationalist-held territories, also in 1926. These congresses called for the overthrow of local despots, for reduction of rent and repayment of 'rent deposits', for the organization of peasant militia for village self-defence and for the liquidation of the landlords' *min-t'uan*. The Peasant Association movement was too widespread and had too much cohesion to have developed spontaneously, even in so favourable a political situation. Although Mao Tse-tung's report is very reticent on this point, there is no doubt that the Peasant Associations were founded, at least in the initial stage, by people from the cities: militant revolutionaries, intellectuals, worker cadres and peasants who had received a political training, especially those who had attended the Peasant Movement Training Institute, established in Canton in 1925 under the direction of Mao Tse-tung. The movement subsequently spread 'like a prairie fire'. Only the influence of external elements, which can be seen again in the case of the Kiangsi soviet in 1930, can explain how the peasants were able to take such a decisive step forwards, to pass from the archaic structure of the secret societies to that of the Peasant Associations – true provisional forms of peasant power in a modern revolutionary situation.

The success of the Peasant Associations was connected with the whole revolutionary upsurge in China between 1924 and 1927. It benefited in particular from the rise of the labour movement: the general strike of textile workers in Shanghai, the strike and boycott in Canton and Hong Kong between June 1925 and October 1926, etc. But the very success of the peasant movement, like that of the labour movement, was to influence the course of the revolution and precipitate a crisis in the Kuomintang-Communist alliance.

The Communist Party supported the peasant movement and maintained that the agrarian question was of decisive importance for the future of the revolution. This was also the policy of the Comintern and of Stalin. It was necessary, Stalin said in November 1926, to rouse millions of peasants in the service of the revolution, and the Central Committee of the Chinese Communist Party, in July the same year, spoke of reinforcing the peasant movement in order to take over its leadership. For strategic and theoretical reasons, however, the Chinese Communists hesitated to give unqualified support and encouragement to the peasant movement. Their strategy gave

37 'Liberate the Chinese people from imperialist generals, bourgeoisie and bureaucrats!' A Russian poster of 1931 voices solidarity with the Chinese Communists.

38 Badge (number 30) belonging to one of the first members of the special committee of the Chinese Communist Party in T'ung-ch'iang.

39 Sun Yat-sen with two Soviet advisers, General Vassily Blücher and I. K. Mamaev; two years after this meeting Blücher was to play a prominent role in Chiang Kai-shek's Northern Expedition.

priority to their alliance with the moderate nationalists and they feared that the primitive vigour of the peasant struggles, such as Mao Tse-tung had observed in Hunan, would frighten their allies, the Kuomintang, the bourgeoisie and the nationalist army. Moreover, the Chinese Communists and their mentors in Moscow were convinced that, even in countries in which there was little industrialization, the notion of the leading role of the industrial proletariat should be taken in the narrowest sense; everything depended upon the struggle in the industrialized cities. The peasants could be no more than a make-weight, or a rear guard (the term used by Liu Shao-ch'i at the Third National Congress of Labour Unions at Canton in May 1926). In the Marxist view of history generally accepted in Moscow, the peasant movement was only a component of the bourgeois-democratic revolution; its supreme objective was private ownership of land – a fundamentally bourgeois aspiration. Such was the experience of the French Revolution of 1789, which was now applied to very different historical conditions.

This is why the agrarian programme of the Communists fell far short of what actually happened in the villages of Hunan and Hailufeng. It envisaged, on the economic side. no more than the limitation of rent and interest rates; on the political side, the peasants should insist on freedom of assembly, organization and the vote, but should not raise the question of power; the struggle should be concentrated against the most reactionary of the landlords, should seek to unite all the peasants, including small and medium landlords; peasant armed self-defence should be held in check by certain restrictions. This was the policy laid down in the resolution of the Central Committee of the C.C.P. in July 1926.

The political line of appeasing the moderates failed in its aim. The Chinese bourgeoisie was much more closely tied to the landlord economy than the Communist strategy had bargained for; it possessed land and a substantial proportion of its revenue was made up of rents. The collusion between the Kuomintang and the privileged classes in the countryside was reinforced by the fact that the latter, as an insurance for the future, encouraged their sons to enlist as officers in the army of the nationalists. The upsurge of the peasant movement in 1926–27, badly led and weakly supported though it was, nevertheless provoked much anxiety among the hesitant allies of the Communists; all the more so because it was accompanied by a similar upsurge in the labour movement, which was also held in check by the Communists for the sake of appeasement, but was nevertheless vigorous, especially in Shanghai, Canton and Wuhan. For Chiang Kai-shek and the leaders of the Kuomintang it was possible, after the success of the Northern Expedition in 1926–27, to dispense with the support of popular forces against the northern militarists. Indeed it became a necessity to dissociate from such allies, whose activities threatened the position of the privileged classes in town and country-side. The peasant upsurge, like that of the labour movement, objectively contributed to the political polarization and the eventual explosion on the revolutionary front which the Communists had been trying to prevent. At Shanghai on 12 April 1927 Chiang Kai-shek broke with the Communist Party and massacred thousands of militant workers.

For several months more, certain elements of the Kuomintang and the nationalist regime, installed at Wuhan, continued to maintain the alliance with the Communists. At this stage the Communist position on the peasant problem became more radical, at least in principle. Without going so far as to call for peasant soviets, as Trotsky proposed, the Chinese Communist Party adopted the slogan 'land to the tillers'; but the value of this new radical policy was immediately and fundamentally weakened by the fact that the land-holdings of officers in the nationalist armies were exempt from confiscation, which meant that land belonging to a large proportion of the gentry could not be touched. A Communist, T'an P'ing-shan, leader of the National Peasant Congress, became Minister of Agriculture in the Wuhan government; but he joined with the Comintern in condemning 'peasant excesses'. Only a few individual voices were raised in protest. The whole tone of Mao Tse-tung's report of Hunan was an indirect criticism of the Communist leaders' attempts to hold the peasant movement in check.

The Communist policy of compromise could not save the revolution. In July the Wuhan government broke with the Communists, and the majority of its members went over to Chiang Kai-shek. White terror had already begun in the countryside of central China where a few months earlier the peasants had been so active and militant. The landlords took heart, reorganized their militia, attacked and massacred the militants of the Peasant Associations. The great wave of peasant struggles suffered a temporary set-back in the countryside, just as the upsurge of the labour movement, which had begun in 1925, suffered defeat in the towns.

6 The Peasant Movement under Communist Leadership 1927–37

The defeat of the revolution in 1927 put an end to the Peasant Association movement; its semi-legal character meant that it could only develop in a favourable, or at least a sufficiently fluctuating, political situation. The wave of white terror launched by the alliance of landlords, warlords and the Kuomintang after 1927 made this kind of struggle impossible. The peasant movement now fell back to more archaic forms of struggle, through the secret societies, spontaneous riots and endemic banditry which, as we have seen, had been very common in the 1920s. At the same time the peasant movement took a decisive step forward in making common cause with the Communist revolutionary movement, which was itself in search of a radical new strategy. Only after 1927 is it possible to speak of a genuine peasant revolution in China; only then did the peasant movement play a role which was more than just marginal to the true revolutionary process, capable of transforming the whole of society and consequently the peasantry itself.

As far as the Communist Party was concerned, this shift to a new strategy was not a matter of choice, but of necessity. The revolution had been crushed in the towns, or abandoned by its allies: in Shanghai in April 1927, Wuhan in July, Nan-ch'ang in August and Canton in December. It was necessary at any price to find a new field of struggle, to move into areas where the enemy was weakest.

At the end of 1927 Mao Tse-tung, on the instructions of the Central Committee, organized an insurrection, the Autumn Harvest Uprising, against the Kuomintang in southern Hunan. He relied on certain units of the nationalist army that had remained faithful to the left and on peasant self-defence militia, formed in the region during the previous year on the initiative of the Peasant Associations. The attempt failed and Mao Tse-tung took refuge in the isolated mountain region of Ching-kang-shan, on the border between Hunan and Kiangsi. Here he was joined by another military group under the leadership of Chu Te, formerly a warlord-minded officer in a warlord army, now turned Communist. Thus the first revolutionary base of the Chinese Red Army was formed.

The process which led the Chinese Communists to the peasantry was an external one; the Communist cadres and the new forms of struggle which they adopted came into the Chinese countryside from outside, from the towns. The essential motivation for this shift was the need to pursue the struggle in the *least unfavourable* conditions possible. The agrarian revolution did not mature in isolation deep within peasant society, but stemmed inevitably from the new strategy which was chosen and became a matter of the highest priority.

The new Communist strategy, therefore, was not elaborated in the abstract. It was initially the fruit of the unfavourable situation which existed in 1927; its theoretical expression came progressively – not only because it involved entirely new practices which developed slowly, but also because the innovators, Mao Tse-tung and Chu Te, were aware of the novelty of their experience and their ideas and avoided formulating them in too clear-cut a manner. This caution, mixed perhaps with a certain timidity with regard to political theory, is shown in their use of vocabulary. At first they did not speak of 'red bases' or 'revolutionary bases' – terms commonly employed later – but of 'bases of support' (*ke-chü ti-ch'ü*, literally 'detached territories'), dissident zones which could be relied on to provide support, implying that these areas of insurgent peasants were only significant in a strategy in which the towns continued to play the central role. The first organs of revolutionary power in these insurgent zones were called soviets – a tribute to the Russian experience of 1917, although the revolutionary process and political content of the Chinese and Russian soviets was very different.

The main elements of this new strategy began to appear in some of Mao Tse-tung's writings, such as *Why Is It That Red Political Power Can Exist in China?* (1928), *The Struggle in the Ching-kang*

40 Mao Tse-tung, who emerged in the late 1920s as the chief advocate of the new Communist strategy of reliance on rural insurgent bases backed by peasant support, rather than on open urban revolt.

Mountains (1928) and *A Single Spark Can Start a Prairie Fire* (1930). The overriding principle was the necessity for armed struggle. The revolution had suffered defeat in 1924–27 because it had no military power at its disposal, and because it was based solely upon the political struggle of the masses – strikes, demonstrations and so on – while the enemy, the Kuomintang, had armed forces at its command. The new military arm of the revolution was the Red Army, originally formed of units of the nationalist army which had rallied to the Communist Party, and joined by peasant volunteers from the insurgent territories.

Armed struggle depended on the existence of geographically limited revolutionary bases, where it was possible to seize power and retain it, without necessarily achieving victory throughout the country. Another difference with the 1917 revolutionary process in Russia was that the insurgent regions in China were necessarily the most backward economically, the least well integrated into the market economy and the most tenuously controlled by the central government; that is to say, the regions most suited to the existence of a dissident movement. This was a major departure from the classical thesis, which assigned the leading role in the revolution to the most evolved zones, where there was modern industry and an industrial proletariat.

It was inevitably the peasantry, rather than the working class, which was called upon to make the main effort. Armed struggle required the mobilization of the peasant masses; but this did not mean that the revolution became no more than a product of the peasant movement and of the special aspirations of the peasantry. It was by an external process that the revolutionary elements, bearers of a new ideology originating with other social classes, came to set the peasants in motion.

The strategy also implied a prolonged struggle. There was no question of seizing power in a few days or hours, no prospect of decisive victory or defeat, as in Paris in 1871, Petrograd in 1917 or Shanghai in 1927. The struggle would last for many years.

Such were the new principles which inspired the revolutionary strategy of the Chinese Communists after 1927, or rather of those Communists who wanted to practise them, since neither the Central Committee, which remained in Shanghai, nor the Comintern really approved of the actions of Mao Tse-tung and Chu Te.

Between 1928 and 1930 eleven main insurgent bases were set up: in Hailufeng west of Canton (the oldest); in the Ching-kang Mountains to which Mao Tse-tung had fled at the end of 1927; the Kiangsi-Fukien base around the town of Jui-chin, capital of the Chinese soviets between 1931 and 1934; that of 'O-yü-wan', from the names of the three provinces of Hopei, Honan and Anhwei on the confines of which it was situated; and the north-western base on the boundaries of Shensi, Kansu and Ninghsia, which became the refuge for the survivors of the Long March, after the other bases had disappeared.

The location of these bases met several geopolitical conditions: they were in areas where enemy administration was weakest, that is to say, in the border areas between provinces, which had always served as refuges for the outlaws of China. In the mountains and forests there were fewer people, state control was tenuous and landlords less powerful. Moreover, because of the inter-provincial rivalries which existed among the new warlords of the Kuomintang, just as they had among the warlords of the 'twenties, it was difficult for them to launch operations from several different directions against these border areas. At the same time, the insurgent zones were within striking distance of the urban centres of the provinces, Nan-ch'ang, Wuhan and Changsha, which they could both dominate and threaten. So a combined revolutionary strategy, based on the coordination of urban uprisings and the participation of guerilla bands of peasants from the mountains, was not precluded. The Central Committee of the C.C.P., which continued to believe in the possibility of powerful revolutionary movements in the towns, had finally accepted, in this situation, the development of the Maoist strategy of insurgent zones.

With a few exceptions these revolutionary bases established in the 'thirties were situated in the south of China, that is to say in areas where the peasant population had already had some political experience. Many had risen in response to the advance of the nationalist army in 1926–27, they had participated in the Peasant Association movement, large numbers had responded to the revolutionary orders of the nationalist government at Canton and later at Wuhan, and had made contact with militant Communists. The peasants of north China, and those of the distant provinces of the south-west, such as Yunnan and Kweichow, had not had the same political experience.

But it would be wrong to suppose that these zones of peasant insurgency were stable and massive territorial entities. Beyond the permanent nuclei, inaccessible to the enemy, were contested areas,

41 *Support for the People's Very Own Army*; a woodcut made in the 1940s illustrates the close ties that have always existed between the peasantry and the Red Army.

with shifting political currents. At the height of their expansion, the revolutionary bases contained a population of perhaps ten million or so; the largest was that of Kiangsi-Fukien, with three million. From 1928 to 1931 they were consolidated from a military point of view and formal political institutions were set up; they enjoyed the support of the poor peasants and even began to implement an economic policy.

The Red Army had been founded by revolutionaries from the towns, left-wing army men, intellectuals and workers – not by peasants. But it was the peasantry that constituted the main source of recruitment, and in particular the peasant self-defence units. Army commanders constantly emphasized the need for maintaining good relations with the peasant masses and winning their confidence. The 'eight rules for the soldier in the countryside' date from this period:

1 Replace all doors when you leave a house;
2 Return and roll up the straw matting on which you sleep;
3 Be courteous and polite to the people and help them when you can;
4 Return all borrowed articles;
5 Replace all damaged articles;
6 Be honest in all transactions with the peasants;
7 Pay for all articles purchased;
8 Be sanitary and, above all, establish latrines a safe distance from people's houses.

Mobilization of the peasantry in the service of the revolution did not mean that the revolution was to take the form of traditional peasant struggles. On the contrary, the peasants could not effectively serve the revolution without breaking completely with the military ways and ideas of the old-style peasant riots. In December 1929 Mao Tse-tung appealed for the 'correction of mistaken ideas in the Party', of which he drew up a highly significant list. He included 'absolute equalitarianism', which he called 'the product of a handicraft and small peasant economy'; a kind of outlaw mentality, connected with the presence in the Red Army of large numbers of 'vagabonds' (*éléments déclassés*); he also castigated 'ultra-democracy' and the 'remnants of putschism'.

In the insurgent bases, the Communists gave priority to the rapid establishment of political institutions and local organs of state power. At first this was done in an empirical manner; but the small-scale provisional governments were soon organized more systematically, in the form of soviets. On 7 November 1931 delegates from the different soviets of south China held a conference at Jui-chin in the Kiangsi-Fukien red base – the date is as significant as the use of the word 'soviet'. Mao Tse-tung became Chairman of the Chinese Soviet Republic which was proclaimed at this conference; the Vice-Chairmen were Hsiang Ying, a textile worker from Shanghai and a veteran of the labour movement, and Chang Kuo-t'ao, an intellectual and one of the founders of the Chinese Communist Party. Peasant representation in the direction of the insurgent areas did not, as we can see, correspond with the importance of their role at the grass-roots.

The Constitution of the Republic affirmed that all power belonged to the workers' soviets. It was marked by a certain formalism: there was clearly a tendency to follow closely the model of the Soviet Constitution of 1924, for instance in the granting of considerable political rights to minorities, including even the right of secession – though in fact there were very few minority peoples in the Chinese soviet regions. The distinction between various categories of electors was also somewhat dogmatic; whereas only 25 workers had the right to elect a delegate to a local soviet, the number of soldiers who had this right was 50 and the number of peasants, 100. This discrimination was all the more unjustified since there was no important industrial complex in the territory of the red bases and their essential social support came from the peasantry.

The labour law was equally formalistic. It provided for an eight-hour day, workers' insurance against sickness, collective agreements and other measures which had been demanded around 1925 by the labour movement in the big cities. Such dogmatism, such artificial emphasis on workers' demands in a region with an overwhelmingly peasant population, showed how fragile the political balance was which held the Kiangsi soviet together. On the one hand, there were the advocates of the policy of red bases, solidly founded upon the peasantry, and, on the other, the protagonists of a more orthodox party apparatus, themselves from the towns, who continued, even in this rural environment which was entirely new to them, to hold that the working class and its demands ought to be the main concern of the revolution. Mao Tse-tung was the Chairman of the Republic of Soviets in Kiangsi, but he seems to have accepted a compromise with the partisans of the opposing line.

The agrarian law, the third key legislative document of the republic, was addressed to a fundamental problem. It envisaged the confiscation, without indemnity, of landlord and feudal land-holdings, and distribution to the poor peasants. This policy, much more radical than that of the Peasant Associations in the preceding period, entailed a systematic effort to determine the class structure of the countryside – a problem dealt with by Mao Tse-tung in his article *How to Differentiate the Classes in the Rural Areas* (1933). It was necessary to distinguish not only the beneficiaries but also the victims of agrarian reform. Poor peasants were those who did not have sufficient land and had to rent more; landlords were those who did not work on the land and who lived comfortably off the work of their tenants. The difficulty lay in defining rich peasants. They had land, and though they lived by exploiting paid labour, theirs was real economic activity. Their land was not to be confiscated, but the general tendency was to regard them with hostility. Mao Tse-tung was very conscious of the risk involved and frequently warned against antagonizing middle-of-the-road elements; but the tendency towards peasant extremism seems to have been too strong, and contributed to the defeat of 1934. Later, Mao Tse-tung described as 'ultra-leftist' the agrarian policy of the Kiangsi soviet period, which left no land for the landlord and bad land for the rich peasants. In 1948 he insisted that these errors should not be repeated, that *individual* means of survival be left to members of classes which *collectively* had to be fought.

The fundamental significance of the Kiangsi Soviet Republic lay in the fusion of the Communist movement with the peasant

42 The hand of the landlord grasps the peasant's land: a woodcut of the mid-1930s symbolizes the exploitation and misery of the peasantry throughout Chinese history.

movement. The establishment of the red bases marked the beginning of a true agrarian revolution. From the arrival in December 1927 of the first armed Communist detachments, according to Chu Te, 'the peasants, thinking the revolutionary bell had tolled, began rising. Soon the small revolutionary army was completely engulfed in a fierce peasant revolution that stretched throughout south Hunan and northern Kwangtung. Peasants arose, attacked the landlords and their *min-t'uan*, and sent desperate calls to Chu Te for men to help them.'

The penetration of the Red Army, the pursuit of armed struggle against the Kuomintang, the establishment of soviet power in the insurgent districts, were only possible because the peasants felt themselves involved. They saw in the Communist revolution the political and military road to their own social liberation, which the old-fashioned riots and the secret societies had been unable to achieve.

The awakening of revolutionary consciousness among the peasantry is expressed, for example, in a popular ballad about the attack of the local Red Army detachments of peasant militia against the walled town of Shan-kang in southern Fukien in September 1929. Once more, in the tradition of peasant revolts, they entered the town, but with perspectives which neither the Red Turbans at Fatshan in 1854, nor the *min-chün* entering Canton in 1911, could have had.

First we must unite and raise the red banner,
second, sew a badge upon our sleeves,
third, destroy reactionaries in the village,
fourth, capture rifles from the landlords –
Arm ourselves!

Enter Shan-kang, disturb no merchants
and always protect the poor;
capture the landlords and tiger gentry –
no compromise with them!
Bandits all!

Never forget the hundred-headed landlords:
militarist, money-lender, magistrate,
tax-collector, police-chief, min-t'uan *leader,*
chamber of commerce and Kuomintang masters,
dog-men all!

Red guards and peasants, be clear!
the date to attack Shan-kang is decided.
We march during the mid-autumn festival.
The man-eating landlords must die!
The people live!

Unfortunately we have no such fascinating accounts of political life in the Kiangsi soviet area as were given by Western visitors to Yenan in the 1940s, when the Communists had moved the peasant guerilla bases northwards in order to resist the Japanese. But the following letter, received and published by the White Russian journalist, V. Yakhontoff, shows that there was a real atmosphere of peasant liberation in the soviet districts, and that the measures of the soviet government, the agrarian law and so on, enjoyed considerable mass support.

At the present time, Sovietized western Fukien is an entirely different world from the rest of the province, where the Kuomintang is still in control. After the victorious revolt the peasants divided the land among themselves and the wages of the workers were raised. The standard of living of the toiling masses has been changed drastically. If previously the poor peasants dreamed of being sons of the rich, the rich ones now would prefer the lot of the poor.

Deeds on land, promissory notes, mortgages and the like all were burnt. The slogan, 'no rent to the landlords, no taxes to the Kuo-min-tang, no payments to the usurers', now became realized. The old collecting agencies are gone, the tax-collectors are shot. Now we are doing our best to help other counties to get rid of the reactionaries, and to start constructive work; to increase production, to improve the irrigation system of the rice fields, to repair the road, to open schools, etc. . . .

The soviet government has started reclamation work. Every peasant now receives enough water for the irrigation of his fields, there are no more quarrels over scarcity of water here . . . in every village we have cooperative societies of consumers and also of producers in some fields. . . . Some of the soviets have founded banks or rather credit associations, where we, the peasants, can borrow money without being robbed by the money-lenders. Usurers are gone.

The attempt to organize the economic life of the insurgent areas was an integral part of the policy of prolonged revolutionary struggle. The bases were to be made capable of providing, for a relatively long period, more or less acceptable conditions for the mass of the peasant population. For their part, the peasants gave moral support to the vanguard fighters and identified themselves with their struggle, without necessarily being ready to accept the same hardships and the same sacrifices. This is why Mao Tse-tung, in his writings of 1933, emphasized the importance of production in the period before the débâcle, when the soviet areas were tending to become stabilized. The main problem at that time was the blockade of each peasant base imposed by the Kuomintang. It was therefore necessary to develop production, not only by cooperatives and mutual-aid teams, but by individual and small-scale activity as well. Even state-organized handicraft production of essential commodities, such as cloth, medicine, farm tools and paper, was started. Mao Tse-tung also recommended, at the Economic Construction Conference held in August 1933 in the south Kiangsi base, a policy of exporting and marketing in the 'white regions' of tungsten, camphor, tobacco, peppermint oil, dried mushrooms and so on – products of the mountainous and forest regions which were greatly in demand in the plains.

The policy of fusion between the Communist movement and the peasant movement, which tended to give precedence to the agrarian revolution, was not supported by the Chinese Communist Party apparatus in general. Mao Tse-tung and Chu Te represented a minority line, if not a marginal one. For the leaders of the Central Committee, which remained in Shanghai, the peasantry continued to be no more than an ally, and the efforts made on their behalf were justified only if the peasantry could be mobilized to attack the industrial cities and support the struggle of the proletariat from outside. This was the strategy of successive leaders of the party in the period which was to follow, and which Ch'ü Ch'iu-pai, Li Li-san and Wang Ming tried to put into practice. They ordered Mao Tse-tung and other leaders of these 'auxiliary bases' to descend into the plains and attack the cities of Wuhan, Changsha and Nan-ch'ang. Their strategy was based on a double error: the labour movement had become too weak to be able to produce such revolutionary

43 *Over the Mountain*, a recent portrayal of an episode in the famous Long March from Kiangsi to Yenan (see map, p. 117).

upsurges as those of 1925–26, while the Kuomintang, on the other hand, was now sufficiently strong militarily, thanks particularly to the aid which it had received from the Western powers, for premature attacks on the cities to be political and military suicide. After several misfortunes, Mao Tse-tung and Chu Te simply refused to execute the directives they received. They were consequently pushed aside by the leaders of the Party and deprived of any political influence. But soon most of the same leaders, defeated in the towns, came to place themselves at the head of the soviet areas.

Such divisions and inconsistencies in the policy of the Communists towards the peasant movement constitute one of the main causes of the final collapse of the Kiangsi soviet. Four successive campaigns of encirclement were beaten off, each time with increasing difficulty. The fifth, in 1934, could not be. Hundreds of thousands of fighters and militants had to set out on the Long March to the north-west. Only a few arrived, between August and November 1935, at Yenan, the small town in Shensi which was to remain the headquarters of Chinese Communism and of the revolution until the fall of the

44, 45 Two sketches made by a fighter on the Long
March: above, *The Hanging Bridge*, a vital crossing-
point taken with great heroism, and, right, *Through
the Mountains*.

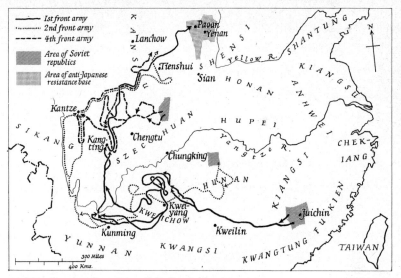

46 Map showing the routes of the Long March.

Kuomintang in 1949. In the middle of the Long March, under the influence of their recent defeat, a critical shake-up in the Communist leadership dislodged the protagonists of the 'left-deviation' – those who wanted to give priority to the urban struggle – and placed Mao Tse-tung and those close to him at the head of the Party.

The period of the Kiangsi soviet was thus a turning point as important for the history of Chinese Communism as it was in the history of the Chinese peasant movement. The fusion of these two currents allowed the development of a real agrarian revolution, capable of giving new historical perspectives and of uprooting the very base of the old political and social regime, instead of merely protesting against its abuses, as the secret societies and spontaneous riots continued to do, even in the 'thirties. But this agrarian revolution was the fruit of an external process, as we have already noted in relating the events of the autumn of 1927, which characterizes the whole period of the Kiangsi soviet. The peasantry was certainly the principal social force on which the struggle against the Kuomintang

47 *The Torch of Yenan*, a modern painting commemorating, in idealized style, the conclusion of the Long March.

depended, but the revolutionary movement had not matured within the peasantry; it had come from outside, driven by the need to pursue the armed struggle in the least unfavourable conditions which could be found. The peasantry was led by men from elsewhere, who had a different kind of political experience. Chu Te, even if he was the son of very poor peasants, had studied in modern schools at the end of the nineteenth century, he had served in the New Army, participated in the revolutionary and republican groups in 1911 and later had become a warlord's officer. The peasantry had been influenced by a modern revolutionary ideology – Marxism – which sought to break with the primitive traditions of egalitarianism and adventurism of the secret societies. The peasantry in the epoch of the Kiangsi soviet was directed by the Red Army and the Communist Party, that is to say, by forms of organization very different from the tradition of the ancient rebellions.

The agrarian revolution, of which the Kiangsi soviet was the first step, relied essentially upon the poor peasantry; it was the heir of the traditional peasant movement and stemmed from the same social roots; but it also implied a rupture with it.

7 Yenan – Peasant Headquarters of the Communist Revolution

In July 1937 the Japanese launched a general invasion of China. Very quickly they seized all the major industrial and railway towns of north China. The Kuomintang took refuge in the distant plateaux and basins of the south-west where for eight years they were content with a military strategy of waiting.

From this moment, the struggles of the Chinese peasants under the leadership of the Chinese Communists changed in character. The strategic principle remained the same – prolonged armed struggle demanding the formation of small insurgent bases, of which the main social base was necessarily the peasantry – but from now on these bases were devoted to resistance against Japan, which took priority over the fight against the landlords and the Kuomintang. The Long March of 1934–35 had been initially a desperate measure to avoid complete liquidation of the peasant soviets of Kiangsi, to save at least the cadres and the future of the peasant revolution. But on arrival in the loess plateau of north-west China, where the Communists took refuge, there occurred a remarkable change in the historical situation. The Communists found themselves in a very favourable flank position, both from a political and a military point of view. They were in a better position than the Kuomintang to keep an eye on Japanese-occupied zones, they were in direct contact with the peasants of north China who were bearing the whole weight of the Japanese occupation and could therefore be mobilized for armed resistance.

From 1937 onwards the Japanese occupied all the major urban centres of north China; but they could not avoid the extension of their operations into the countryside, and a clash with the peasantry. They had to recruit by force the civil labour and military auxiliaries they needed, in particular the 'puppet troops', officially commanded by the pro-Japanese government installed in Nanking. They were forced to react against the latent hostility of the population and organize the suppression of the guerilla bands which were beginning to form. Japanese mopping-up campaigns, the measures of the 'rural pacification movement', and, above all, the extermination campaigns became more and more harsh as peasant resistance developed. In 1942 the Japanese General Okamura formulated his policy of *Sanko Seisaku* ('three alls' –burn all, kill all and destroy all). The very severity of the Japanese occupation left the peasants no choice but to rise up on a mass scale.

A Communist tract distributed to the peasants of the north in September 1938 declared:

Comrades! Japan has invaded our Shansi, killed large numbers of our people, burned thousands of our houses, raped our women in countless numbers, robbed us of our food and wealth, trampled on the graves of our ancestors, forced our wives and children to flee, destroyed our famous places. . . . Everybody! Rise up and join a guerilla self-defence unit! Exterminate the Peace Maintenance Committee which sells out the nation! Defend our anti-Japanese patriotic people's government! Assist the all-out resistance of Commander Yen [Hsi-shan]! Act in unison with Army and people to overthrow Japanese imperialism!

(The Peace Maintenance Committee was a collaborationist organization in this area. Yen Hsi-shan was the warlord ruler of Shansi Province, to whom the Communists gave tactical support against Japan.)

That the mobilization of the peasantry and their support for the Communist guerillas was based on the national will to resist is shown by the development of a new political vocabulary. The peasants, from the time the Japanese arrived to occupy their villages, were familiar with such terms – and the ideas which they represented – as *chiu-kuo* (national salvation), *han-chien* (traitor or collaborator), *wei-chün* (puppet army), *Ji-k'ou* (Japanese bandits).

48 Japanese troops enter Peking in July 1937 at the beginning of the eight-year war with China.

The latent and spontaneous hostility of the peasantry towards the Japanese invaders would not have found historical expression if it had not been for the existence of an organizing force – the Communist survivors of the Long March. From 1938 onwards the Eighth Route Army (the name adopted by the Communist forces in the north-west after the agreement reached with the Kuomintang in July 1937 to resist Japan) organized guerilla bases in the Japanese rear. The Shansi-Chahar-Hopei base was around the Wu-t'ai Mountains; the Shansi-Hopei-Shantung-Honan base was in the region of the T'ai-hang Mountains; another base, that of Shansi-Suiyuan, was on the edge of the desert in the north-west; other bases were in east Shantung and the lower Yangtze. All these bases, like that of Shensi-Kansu-Ninghsia, which the Communists had established after their arrival at Yenan after the Long March, were situated, as

49 A unit of the Eighth Route Army advances through the Wu-t'ai Mountains to attack the Japanese rear.

their names indicate, on inter-provincial boundaries, in areas which were relatively easy to defend. They conformed to the ancient geopolitical law of peasant insurrection, of which the Nien, for example, had proved the value. The bases were officially called 'Border Regions' (*pien-ch'ü*).

For eight years, armed struggle against Japan was carried on by these guerilla bases under extremely difficult conditions. The Japanese enjoyed absolute superiority in heavy equipment, such as artillery, armoured vehicles and the like; but the Communists had the advantage of a very flexible organization on three levels: the regular army, the peasant militia and the local guerillas. Their high degree of mobility, the ease with which they could obtain supplies from the towns, their excellent intelligence system – in sum, the constant support they received from the peasantry – allowed them to evade Japanese attempts to surround them, to survive the 'mopping-up', 'nibbling-up' and 'village-combing' campaigns, and even take the offensive. Together with the Vietnamese resistance against the French in 1946–54 and, since 1965, against the American forces, the Communist-led struggle against Japan is one of the most perfect examples of a 'people's war', based on the intimate unity of the armed forces with a peasant population which gives them complete *political* and therefore military support.

The demands of the agrarian revolution were temporarily subordinated to the resistance against Japan and the policy of 'national salvation'. New broad political alliances became necessary, although the poor peasantry of north China continued to be the main social base for the Communist movement. The theory behind these new alliances was propounded by Mao Tse-tung in 1940 in his article *On New Democracy*; they were to constitute a new form of political structure, different from both 'bourgeois democracy' and the Soviet type of democratic socialism. 'New democracy' was based on the alliance of the 'four revolutionary classes' – the proletariat, the poor and middle peasants, the petty bourgeoisie (including intellectuals and so on) and the 'national capitalists'. These four classes were associated together in the same historical mission: to defeat imperialism – by fighting the Japanese – and to destroy feudalism. In the 'liberated areas' controlled by the guerillas, political power was organized on this basis. Local governments were set up on the 'three-three-three' principle: that is, three Communists, three members of the centre parties (eventually including the Kuomintang) and three non-party progressives. Indeed, the political alliance went even further, and landlords were encouraged to participate actively in the struggle against Japan, in spite of their social position as the natural enemies of the peasants. Priority given to resistance against Japan made them at least temporary allies of the peasantry; hence the term 'enlightened landlords' (*k'ai-ming ti-chu*), which underlined the necessity of an alliance between the poor peasantry and their age-old adversaries.

It has been argued that during the war against Japan patriotic motives simply replaced the aims of the social struggle in the minds of the peasants, that they were willing to renounce the struggle against landlords and the feudal order, and that it was 'peasant nationalism' which in the end defeated Japan and brought the Communists to power. This theory claims that the Communists were defeated during the Kiangsi period, when their strategy was based on the agrarian revolution, and that success came only when they became the leaders of the national resistance against Japan, when they became astute enough to direct a hitherto abortive peasant movement on to a new course. Such is the thesis, put forward in a somewhat sensational form, by Chalmers Johnson in his *Peasant Nationalism and Communist Power*.

It is true that the agreements of July 1937 between the Communists and the Kuomintang meant applying a brake to the agrarian revolution, in theory at least. Temporarily, for the sake of unity against Japan, the Communists agreed to renounce their radical agrarian policy and the confiscation of landlords' holding without compensation; but in exchange they obtained from the Kuomintang a fundamental concession – the right to preserve their own armed forces, the Eighth Route Army and the New Fourth Army, to fight against Japan. This meant, in effect, the right of the peasants to keep their arms, and the possibility of continuing at a later date their struggle for land.

50 Building a war-time airfield by hand.

51, 52 Wooden blocks used for printing 'resistance currency' for circulation in a guerilla base: the Communists were early advocates of a Romanized alphabet.

53 Contemporary Japanese view of Chinese guerilla activity in Manchuria.

54 Destroying a captured enemy stronghold.

55 Peasants immobilize an enemy-controlled railway track, part of the guerilla operations behind the Japanese lines.

During the war, Communist agrarian policy in the liberated zones and guerilla bases was one of calculated moderation. Its essential elements were the reduction of land rent (by 25 per cent) and the limitation of interest on loans 'to a reasonable level', which would neither ruin the debtor nor discourage the potential creditor. Particular emphasis was put on production, and the 'production campaigns' of 1938 and 1941–42 aimed at making the liberated areas self-sufficient. In the Shensi-Kansu-Ninghsia Border Region cultivated land increased from 9 million *mou* in 1936 to $12\frac{1}{2}$ million in 1942.

It would be quite wrong to consider that the period of the anti-Japanese resistance was one of retreat for the peasant movement. The policy of rent and interest reduction was pursued with vigour, with the deliberate intention of reducing the economic power of the landlords. In Shansi, for example, where many peasants had fallen heavily into debt during the agricultural depression of the 'thirties, interest rates were fixed at 10 per cent, and the families of soldiers in the people's army, that is to say the poorest families, enjoyed a complete moratorium on their debts. The fiscal policy of the popular committees set up in the liberated areas was also very hard on the landlords. Taxes paid by peasants were considerably reduced, if not completely abolished; those paid by landlords were increased, in accordance with the slogan, 'Those with wealth must contribute money, those with muscle – their strength' – a new form of the ancient slogan of peasant rebels, 'Hit the rich and help the poor!'

Even more important is the fact that the development of armed resistance against Japan led to a radical change in the political balance of power between the gentry and the poor peasants, even if this was not at the time the result of radical land reform measures. Taking arms against Japan and contributing the main war effort, the peasants inevitably became conscious of their historical power and developed confidence in their own strength. They knew, and the landlords knew as well, that their arms could serve in the future to defend their class interests and not just their country. Moreover, because of the traditional solidarity of the 'forces of law and order' and the fear of compromising their material interests, the gentry naturally tended to collaborate with the enemy, or at least to maintain a policy of 'wait and see'. 'Enlightened landlords' were exceptional and although the emphasis between 1937 and 1945 was upon patriotic resistance to Japan rather than on the social struggle, the peasants often found themselves in the opposite camp to the landlords. In the final analysis the term 'collaborator' had as much a class significance as a patriotic one.

Even if the temporary needs of political strategy led to a postponement of the agrarian revolution, the Chinese Communist Party remained, in the eyes of the peasants of north China, the party of the poor. The peasantry of Shansi called the Eighth Route Army 'the good army that does not harm people or do evil things', 'our army, the army of the poor'.

During the eight years of resistance against Japan, a real 'social model' was created at Yenan and in the other Border Regions. It was the image of a new society founded on new political and human relations, with a new culture and a new type of militant revolutionary. It was a rural society, and the fruit of peasant struggles. The headquarters of the Chinese revolution was henceforth a peasant headquarters, and remained so until 1949.

The peasant society of Yenan was a military society, in which armed resistance was closely integrated with the everyday life of everyone, and in which the traditional aspects of peasant life were adapted for military purposes. The land was dug, not merely for planting crops, but also for making tunnels and planting mines; munitions, and not just the harvest, were transported in the peasants' carts; children might be sent from village to village to carry messages concerning guerilla action and not just to transmit village or family gossip. Peasants are accustomed to keep quiet about what goes on in their heads, so they knew how to keep quiet about the movements of the Eighth Route Army. The American journalist, Harrison Forman, who visited the liberated zones of north China in 1944, wrote:

That village was one of the most belligerent I have ever seen. Every approach, every trail, was heavily mined; and the mines

56 View of Yenan, ultimate destination of the Long March, and Communist headquarters during both the war with Japan and the succeeding civil war.

were set not only on the trails but also in the fields, where the wary Japs might be expected to move. This was a precaution against possible Jap reinforcements. Warning notices, easy to remove should the enemy approach, were stuck into the ground over every mine. It gave you a goose-pimply sensation to zigzag your horse carefully in and out between those marked mines – you hoped they hadn't missed marking any!

Even the village entry was mined. The villagers moved about nonchalantly, as though oblivious of death underfoot. Every one carried a weapon of some sort – a rifle over his back, a potato-masher grenade at his hip. This weapon carrying had grown so natural that even the little boys and girls wore dummy grenades dangling from their waists.

In pre-war days, this village was locally famed for the manufacture of firecrackers, and the inhabitants had now turned their firecracker-making skill to the making of mines. In one courtyard I saw men, women and children at work making black powder, casting mine-molds, and piling-up loaded mines in neat heaps. Because of the shortage of metal for the mine-casings, some of the villagers were hollowing out big rocks to make stone mines; others were filling bottles, jugs, and even teapots; and one man was fashioning a wooden cannon of his own invention.

The significance of all this lay not in the effectiveness of such primitive weapons; it lay in their clear reflection of the fighting spirit of the people. A people must needs be brave who would match such puny contrivances against the deadly weapons of the enemy.

The society of Yenan was also a democratic society, in which the traditional opposition between the organs of power – military as well as civil – and more recently between members of the Party and ordinary people was reduced to the minimum. The civil and military cadres shared the simple life of the peasants and soldiers, lived like them in caves cut out of the loess hills, and bore no insignia of rank or power. The army was profoundly linked with the peasantry; not only because it enjoyed their constant support in military operations and drew recruits from the villages, but also because the army helped with work in the fields, instead of living at the expense of the villages like the armies of the past. As the journalist Israel Epstein wrote in the *Calcutta Statesman* and the *New York Times*,

The tax burden of the peasantry is reduced because garrison troops, the personnel of government institutions, university students and other similar groups have all been given waste land to cultivate, and produce at least a part of their food themselves, lessening the dependence on the grain levy. An Eighth Army brigade which we visited had reclaimed 25,000 acres and was growing more than twice the amount of food and cotton it required. The surplus was

135

sold to the government or on the market, and the proceeds were equally divided among the men in accordance with the number of work-days they had put in.

The Eighth Route Army, from company upwards, has elected economic committees which supervise rations, the proper expenditure of mess money and so forth. Officers and men sit on these committees on equal terms, and the committees, which must produce their accounts on the demand of any soldier, see that every one shares equally from the production of the unit. . . .

The same kind of equality was to be found in the relationships between men and women. Except for those who had joined secret societies in the old days, peasant women had always been kept in a situation of family dependence and social subordination. Now they participated actively in the work of the peasant committees, in guerilla operations, in the production campaigns; they formed their own groups, the Women's Associations, the better to mobilize and keep an eye open for the recurrence of 'male chauvinism'.

The atmosphere of close unity between the people and its organized advance guard, the army and Party owed its existence to the deep crisis which shook the Communist Party between 1940 and 1942, in the 'rectification campaign'. The object of this was to teach Communists to break with élitist practices, with the dogmatism and sectarianism of the Comintern period, with the habit of relying on authoritarian measures and ready-made formulas. Mao Tse-tung said in 1938, '. . . empty and abstract talk must be stopped and doctrinairism must be buried to make way for the fresh and lively things of Chinese style and Chinese flavour which the common folk of China love to see and hear.'

The revolutionary militants from the towns, the intellectuals and cadres, had to go to the school of the peasantry, to learn its language and to draw on its rich traditions and colourful imagery. The 'rectification' of the Communist Party was accompanied by the elaboration of a new popular culture, fed by peasant tradition and at the same time integrated with the revolutionary struggle. The vitality of this new culture was one of the characteristics of the

57, 58 Daily life in Yenan: above, spinning cotton, part of the campaign to achieve industrial self-sufficiency in the liberated areas; below, Mao Tse-tung chats with peasants.

Yenan period. In 1942 a forum of writers and artists was held there, at which intellectuals were encouraged to form closer links with the ordinary peasants, to live among them and express their aspirations. Several writers came from Shanghai or other great cities, completely ignorant of peasant life, and in response to this call immersed themselves in village life and took part in one way or another in the revolutionary struggles of the time. But no one captured the atmosphere of rural life better than Chao Shu-li. His book, *The Rhymes of Li Yu-tsai* (1943), portrays a sharp and perceptive peasant, who observes in silence the oppression of the peasants by the landlords, the peculations of the village bigwigs and the errors of inexperienced Communist cadres; but in the rhymes which he improvises he poses discreetly yet trenchantly the political problems which the peasants must themselves understand before they can resolve them. He appeals, for example, for others to join the recently founded peasant association, the only force in the village able to destroy the hidden power of the privileged:

> *Join the Peasants' Union; it will make us stronger.*
> *Anybody cheats us, we can fetch him a good crack.*
> *Old Yen can't now press us any longer.*
> *All the stolen land back, all the squeezed cash back;*
> *Reduce all the rents to the last squeezed penny;*
> *Out with officials who want to get us on the run.*
> *We're going to be tough with them, we aren't having any.*
> *Join the Peasants' Union if you want to see it done.*

Old Yen in this novel was the biggest landlord and usurer in the village, who was also made mayor by the Kuomintang.

Another expression of this revolutionary peasant culture is found in the woodcuts, employing simple tools and rough paper, which were produced in great quantities in the Yenan period. They portrayed labour in the fields, the terror of Japanese occupation, the heroism of the partisans and the hope of a better society.

It was at Yenan that the first blueprints were made of a new kind of Chinese society, primitive to be sure, but militant and cultivated as well. Some of the best-known Chinese intellectuals, such as the historian Fan Wen-lan, taught at K'ang-ta – the Anti-Japanese Resistance University. They shared, as did the leaders of the Communist Party and the army, the simple and frugal life of the north China peasants; they ate gruel made of millet or kaoliang more often than flour noodles or rice; they drank boiled water more often than tea. Yenan society was founded on political and economic values entirely different from those of the cities. It was influenced more by the tradition of the ancient peasant movements than by the workers' struggles of the 1920s. It was never completely cut off from the outside world, since Japanese, Korean and Vietnamese revolutionaries (including Ho Chi-minh) came to Yenan; so did Western progressives such as Norman Bethune, the Canadian surgeon, who gave his skill and his life to the guerilla bases. The style of collective, community life was expressed in the symbolic dance called the *yang-ko*, well known to all who lived in the liberated areas. It was without any complicated steps or rhythms, but expressed by the simple and expressive movements of the body the feeling that the dancers belonged to the same social organism, the same historic movement.

Yenan was not a return to some idealized, pre-industrial rural life, it was not an escape from the hard realities of the twentieth century. If the peasantry became the main social support of the Communist revolution, if in taking refuge deep in the fertile 'yellow earth' the Communists found the strength to recover from the defeat of the Kiangsi soviet, it was because the peasantry and the land itself had become an integral part of Communist strategy and Marxist ideology. The peasant movement had been able to fuse so perfectly into the Chinese revolution only by overcoming its own limitations, since the catalyst which had started the movement was the military and economic expansion of the great industrial powers of the twentieth century, and the resistance to this expansion was led by the organized forces which came from outside the rural world, the Communist Party and the Red Army.

In 1945, at the time of the Japanese collapse, the liberated areas had a total area of some 950,000 square kilometres and a population of nearly a million; the regular army was 950,000 strong and the militia 2,200,000 strong, while the village self-defence units could boast ten millions. There were nineteen liberated areas. The oldest and strongest were in north China: the Shansi-Kansu-Ninghsia Border Region, with the Central Committee and the Central Revolutionary Military Commission at Yenan; other liberated areas in the north were bounded by the railway network of the region, and directly threatened the cities of Peking, Tientsin, Paoting, Taiyuan and so forth. The liberated areas of central China were located in the valleys of the Yangtze and its tributaries; they were less extensive and politically less stable. In south China there were two small guerilla zones, one in the hinterland of Canton and the other on the island of Hainan.

In comparison with the period between 1935 and 1937, the situation had turned in favour of the Chinese revolutionary movement. The Communists now had considerable political and military power and were in a position to play a decisive role in Chinese politics. They nevertheless sought first of all a political solution. Mao Tsetung, who visited Chiang Kai-shek in Chungking in October 1945, and Chou En-lai, who resided in Nanking as soon as the nationalist government returned there, attempted to arrive at a formula for a coalition government, which both the Kuomintang and the Americans favoured, at least in principle. But disagreement was fundamental. The Kuomintang insisted that the armed forces of the Communists must be disbanded before they could be allowed to share power. The Communists insisted on preserving their armed forces, which they regarded as the sole guarantee of real democratization of Chinese political life and the end of Kuomintang dictatorship. At most, as a last attempt at conciliation, the Communists agreed to evacuate their armies from eight of the liberated areas which they controlled at the time of the Japanese surrender, those in the south. But civil war was resumed in July 1946, and the participation of the peasantry, right up until the final defeat of the Kuomintang in 1949, was to be as large-scale and as decisive as it had been in the war of resistance against Japan.

In the new political situation the Communists no longer had any reason to subordinate the aims of the agrarian revolution to the exigencies of the united front and national resistance to Japan, as they had been obliged to do between 1937 and 1945. On the contrary, it was now indispensable to mobilize the peasantry more widely than ever before to fight against the Kuomintang and its landlord allies in the countryside. An official directive in May 1946 and the agrarian programme of October 1947 prepared the way for the concentration of forces in the areas under Communist control and the renewal of the class struggle of the poor peasantry. The significance of these two documents lies in the fact that they gave expression to the political situation as it was, to the upsurge of a semi-spontaneous popular movement, one which was, at the same time, led and encouraged by the Communist Party. The new revolutionary wave has been vividly described in accounts by foreigners sympathetic to the Chinese revolution, who lived in the liberated areas and in the villages and saw the development of peasant struggles, in Isabel and David Crook's *Revolution in a Chinese Village*, in *China Shakes the World* by Jack Belden, and above all in William Hinton's *Fanshen, A Documentary of Revolution in a Chinese Village*.

These accounts show that legislative measures for land reform decided upon by the authorities in the liberated areas would have been inoperative if they had not coincided with a political offensive of the poor peasants against the landlords: confiscation of their property, public 'accusation meetings' and 'speak bitterness' meetings, the pursuit of accomplices and 'running dogs', especially of those who hid goods for the landlords against another day, the search for concealed wealth and luxury goods, the destruction of land deeds – activities which often involved brutality and eventually summary executions.

What Engels called 'the robust violence' of the peasantry was nourished by the age-old hatred of the slaves of the land for those who lived off their misery, by the memories of the Japanese occupation and their landlord collaborators.

The peasants took revenge for countless humiliations and miseries by primitive violence, by the brutality with which they treated the accused landlords. Their confiscation of goods and luxuries from the houses of the rich was symbolic of the revenge of the exploited upon the exploiters. Liberation consisted above all in the fact of speaking up, of expressing oneself, of having the moral courage to stand up to the enemy. The peasants became conscious of their collective strength through reasoned examination of the condition of each one of them. Jack Belden described how villagers settled accounts with a landlord called Wang:

> Suddenly, someone said: 'Maybe Wang will run away.'
> 'Let's get him tonight,' said several farmers at once.
> After some discussion, they all trooped out of the cave and started a march on Landlord Wang's home. Among the thirty men, there was one rifle and three hand grenades.
> The marching farmers separated into two groups. One climbed on the top of the cliffs and worked along the cave roofs until they were over the courtyard. Others marched directly to the gate, knocked loudly and commanded the landlord to open up.

59 A peasant settles accounts with his landlord; in the campaign for land reform legislative measures were combined with political action, and peasants were encouraged to speak out their bitterness towards their landlords.

60 A People's Court in session: the establishment of courts such as these, where cases were tried by the local community, formed an important part of the self-liberation of the peasantry.

Wang's wife answered the door and announced that her husband was not at home. Refusing to believe her, the peasants made a search and discovered a secret passage behind a cupboard. Descending through an underground tunnel, they found Wang cowering in a subterranean cave. They took him away and locked him up overnight. . . .

In the course of the morning and afternoon, the crowd accused the landlord of many crimes, including betrayal of resistance members to the Japanese, robbing them of grain, forcing them into labour gangs. At last he was asked if he admitted the accusations.

'All these things I have done,' he said, 'but really it was not myself who did it, but the Japanese.'

He could not have chosen worse words. Over the fields now sounded an angry roar, as of the sea, and the crowd broke into a wild fury. Everybody shouted at once, proclaiming against the landlord's words. Even the non-participating bystanders warmed to something akin to anger.

Then above the tumult of the crowd came a voice louder than the rest, shouting: 'Hang him up!'

The chairman of the meeting and the cadres were disregarded. For all that the crowd noticed they did not exist.

The crowd boiled around Wang, and somewhere a rope went swishing over a tree. . . .

In this incident the anger of the peasants had not merely been aroused by the memory of all the crimes and exactions of the Wangs as landlords and collaborators; it stemmed also from the discovery of the murderer of Old Li, one of the first peasants who had dared to speak out when the others were still silent.

The reaction of the landlords to peasant anger was both brutal and cunning, and always very determined – the resistance of a privileged class with centuries of experience. This was real class struggle, carried on without mercy. The landlords attempted to corrupt the most determined of the peasants, to seduce them by means of their daughters or young servants, to intimidate them by sorcery and superstition and by assassinating cadres from the towns. The land-lords hid their goods, recruited peasants by terror and attempted to slander the militants by nosing into their pasts.

The agrarian reforms of May 1946 and October 1947 took place against this background of collective violence and the awakening of the consciousness of the oppressed. The directive of May 1946 returned to the slogan of 'land to the tiller'; landlords' holdings were compulsorily purchased, not with money, but by bonds issued by the local governments of the liberated areas. Heavier taxes were imposed, and reduction of land rent applied retroactively, so that landlords were obliged to pay back considerable sums to their tenants. By themselves these measures did not change the relations of production in the countryside; but combined with the mass struggles about which we have spoken above, they implied a return to agrarian radicalism.

The land programme of October 1947 completed this evolution. All debts were written off without compensation and landlords' ownership rights were annulled. Their lands and other goods became the property of the Poor Peasants' Association, for distribution to the peasants. The rich peasants only had their surplus land confiscated. Clearly the Communists were still on their guard against 'left excesses', that is to say, against the killing of landlords, looting, violent attacks on rich and even middle peasants. In an article dated February 1948 Mao Tse-tung called for 'correction of leftist deviations in land reform propaganda'. He condemned excessively harsh measures against rich peasants, in order to preserve the political alliance with marginal elements and safeguard production and the economic balance of the liberated areas. References were still made (by Mao Tse-tung in March 1948, for example) to 'enlightened landlords', rural gentry who supported the political struggle of the Communists against the Kuomintang as they had supported them against the Japanese, which shows that priority was still given to political objectives.

The same flexibility of approach can be seen in the distinction between 'old liberated areas' and 'new liberated areas'. Radical agrarian policies were applied only in the former, where the peasant movement had strong roots. In areas recently conquered by the Communist armies in the course of the war against the Kuomintang, there was only reduction of rents and interest rates on loans, measures which would not preclude the development of a real political movement among the peasantry. But the essential trend was that of return to agrarian radicalism. One hundred million peasants received the land upon which they and their ancestors had toiled. In the villages social, moral and political relationships were fundamentally transformed, and this was of greater significance than a mere change in land ownership.

Throughout these violent agrarian struggles between 1946 and 1948 the emphasis upon 'changing man' was more marked than during the Yenan period and the war of resistance against Japan. The idea of *fan-shen* (literally, to turn over the body) is almost an exact parallel to St Paul's 'put off the old man and put on the new'. The term *fan-shen* was used of peasants who dared look the landlords in the face, who dared to stand up against their power and prestige. It was also applied to Communist cadres. Towards 1947–48 there was a natural recrudescence of bureaucratic practices in the liberated areas. Some of the peasant militants who had become cadres tended to abuse their power, to enrich themselves and to engage in intrigue; they had arms and were inclined to take privileges for themselves. According to William Hinton,

> The style of work that developed out of the cadres' attempt to 'keep things moving' in spite of this growing rift was called 'commandism'. Without realizing what was actually happening, many leading cadres in Long Bow began to issue orders instead of educating and persuading people, and because most people obeyed these orders – some because they too thought the redundant attacks necessary, some because they always followed orders, and some because they dared not do otherwise – the leaders did not realize how much support they had lost. The peasants who did not obey they condemned as backward – *suan liu liu te*, or 'sour and slippery' trouble-makers who needed to be taught a lesson. Some of these were arrested, beaten, and punished with extra work for soldiers' families, or extra terms of rear service such as stretcher bearing or transporting supplies to the front. Some were even sent off to join the army, but since they went unwillingly the army wisely rejected them. . . .
>
> Did these leaders, who had climbed from the mud and slime and still carried with them the stains of their origin, possess the vision and the skill to correct the excesses that marred the movement? Could they abolish petty advantages won through the lever of leadership, lead all the poor to stand up, and unite the whole population around that vast program of private, mutual and public production which alone could lift the village of Long Bow out of the miasma of the past? And if they did not possess such vision and skill, who did?

This is why the Communist Party, whose initiatives coincided with the impatience of the ordinary peasants, launched a 'purification'

61 Mao Tse-tung on the march with the army in northern Shensi, 1947.

campaign. Each cadre came up before public examination by the people under his administration and only the ones who 'passed the gate' were confirmed in their jobs. This internal shake-up in the Party was a foretaste, on a smaller scale, of the violent 'rectifications' of the Cultural Revolution twenty years later.

Without the explosions of the peasant struggle in the liberated areas in 1946–48 the Communist armies would not have been able to hold out against the Kuomintang, whose military superiority had even enabled them to take Yenan and hold it for a time in 1947; nor would they have been able to launch their great counter-offensive of 1948. The same principles of 'people's war' as had been proved in resistance against Japan were now put in operation against Chiang

147

Kai-shek: cooperation between the regular army, guerilla and militia units, the dialectic of 'the fish and the water', deep politicization of the army and so forth. The Kuomintang was progressively driven out of all the rural areas of north China towards the end of 1948 and the major cities were then surrounded.

The military success of the Communists had been greatly facilitated by internal crisis within Kuomintang-held territory, in which there were strikes, student unrest and political discontent among the middle class. For the first time in several decades, the peasant movement was able to coordinate its action effectively with that of other social forces.

However, the very rapidity of the Kuomintang débâcle in 1948–49 created regional, geopolitical distortions which the People's Republic was to inherit. In the rural regions of the north the popular regime was the result of the bitter struggle which had been conducted for ten or fifteen years by the poor peasants against Japan, against the Kuomintang and against the landlords. Consequently its mass base was very solid. But Communist power in the 'new liberated areas' in the south, and in the cities and towns, was the fruit of a sudden victory which was almost premature. It had not been based on the slow accumulation of popular energy in the course of a prolonged struggle, on the gradual maturing of an internal situation leading to the radical defeat of the enemy and the destruction of his social base. The imbalance which resulted from this was still evident much later: the Cultural Revolution was most active in the 'old liberated areas'. The revolutionary process was more painful and slower in regions like Hunan or Szechuan, where Communist power had been established in 1949 on the basis of a sudden rallying of the middle and even of the privileged classes, and not as the result of a prolonged political and military struggle at village level. The transfer of power here had operated directly at the provincial level.

In the spring of 1949, after twenty years of struggle in the countryside, the Communists returned to the towns. Robert Guillain, correspondent of *Le Monde*, who watched their peasant armies enter Shanghai, marching at dawn past the luxurious shops in Nanking Road, imagined the arrival of Martians.

On 1 October 1949 Mao Tse-tung proclaimed the foundation of the People's Republic of China. The Chinese peasantry, whose fight for liberation through the ages had been so many times and so bloodily defeated, now stood among the victors; not as marginal and mistrusted allies, rapidly to be pushed aside as they had been in 1911, but as the main social force of the revolutionary movement. The feudal system of peasant exploitation had survived in the countryside after the fall of the Ch'ing dynasty and the imperial regime, and this agrarian conservatism had condemned the republican revolution to failure. It was the collapse of the feudal regime, consummated by the struggle of the peasants themselves in their villages, which had paved the way and made inevitable the collapse of the Kuomintang.

62 Mao Tse-tung dominates this stamp, issued in 1950, marking the foundation of the People's Republic of China.

8   The Chinese Peasantry and the Modern Chinese Revolution

For twenty-two years the Chinese peasantry was the main 'sphere of influence' of the Chinese Communist Party. After the defeat of the workers' movements of Shanghai, Canton and Wuhan in 1927, and until the entry of the guerillas into the great cities in 1949, the peasantry had provided the main effort in the strategy of armed revolution. Much has been written, sometimes in a superficial, sometimes in a doctrinaire manner, on what would appear to be a major 'Maoist' departure from orthodox Marxism. For certain 'specialists', notably in the United States, the Communists succeeded in seizing power simply by renouncing the principle of the political hegemony of the industrial proletariat, which had hitherto been considered as the only revolutionary class capable of overthrowing capitalism and establishing socialism; the success of Mao Tse-tung constituted an ideological rupture with the tradition of Western workers' movements and with the historical experience of the industrialized countries; the peasantry has now become the principal force of the revolution in the underdeveloped countries.

This argument is perhaps convenient, but it is oversimplified. Mao Tse-tung made important innovations, but the historical relationship established under his direction between the peasant movement and the socialist revolution is a complex one. After 1927, it is true, the centre of gravity of the revolutionary struggle moved to the country-side – to the Kiangsi soviet in 1927–34, to the anti-Japanese bases between 1937 and 1945, and to the old and new liberated areas which surrounded Kuomintang-held cities in 1946–49. But this massive intervention of the peasantry in the process of revolution could only have been accomplished by external stimulation. The ideas, the men, the organizational forms which set the peasantry in motion between

1927 and 1949 came from the towns, from the modern world. Socialism, the concept of 'national salvation', of the struggle against imperialism, of revolution itself, were entirely absent from the ideological spectrum of traditional peasant struggles. Neither throughout the centuries nor at the beginning of the twentieth century had peasant insurgency expressed more than a confused dream of egalitarianism, primitive brotherhood, messianism and millenarianism, justice and good government. The traditional ideology of the secret societies, of the Taipings and of other peasant risings, was rooted in the distant past; the new ideas which came from the towns led the peasants to think about their future.

The men who led the peasant movement after 1926–27 themselves came from outside. Many of the cadres of the Chinese soviets, of the Red Army and of the administrative committees of the liberated areas, were professional revolutionaries, intellectuals, sometimes workers – survivors of the 1927 débâcle. As for the organizational forms of the peasant movement during these twenty-two years, they too differed no less radically from the traditional forms of peasant defiance. These, as we have seen in Chapter 4, had been characterized by explosive but highly unstable, spontaneous mass violence, with riots and attacks on *yamen*, for instance; they had been typified by rigid discipline within the select ranks of the secret societies – Triads, Red Spears, Elder Brother Society and so on. After 1927 peasants were mobilized *en masse* in the Red Army, in guerilla or militia units, in the Communist Party, in the Poor Peasants' Union, poor peasants' committees, in the Women's Associations – all organizational forms which, like their names, had been introduced into peasant society from the outside. The essential ingredients of the modern Chinese revolution – ideas, men and structures – had been initially a product not of the countryside but of the industrial towns, though these new revolutionary forces had themselves only been transformed and adapted as a result of the defeat of the urban revolution in 1927. Implanted in the countryside from then onwards, they allowed the peasant movement to merge with the modern Chinese revolution and provided it with a mass base and a new vigour.

The peasant movement, as an essential part of the Communist revolution after 1927, was not the product of internal and spontaneous evolution of the peasantry itself. The study of twentieth-century China does not confirm the theory of Franz Fanon and his followers that the peasantry is a kind of inherently revolutionary class. The peasants have not acted as an independent historical force. In the last analysis, political hegemony has continued to belong to those forces in the historical process which have succeeded in setting the peasantry in motion; that is to say, the Communist movement with its proletarian roots and proletarian ideology, with its party and army – the instruments of modern revolutionary struggle.

Once the fundamental historical relationship between the peasant movement and the Communist revolution after 1927 is defined in terms of dependence and enrichment, it is not difficult to see that the Chinese peasantry was on the one hand handicapped by some of its traditional characteristics, but also benefited, paradoxically, from its privileged position in the revolution. We have seen (in Chapter 5) that Chinese peasants in the twentieth century preserved a number of characteristics inherited from pre-industrial society. They remained influenced by the backward ideology of primitive struggle, their political horizons remained geographically limited; they were still spontaneously attached to petit-bourgeois private ownership, and they tended, when left to themselves, to revolt only against abuses and injustice rather than against the social system as a whole. These tendencies, which some call 'conservative' or 'counter-revolutionary', were actively combated by the Communists, as can be seen in the works of Mao Tse-tung, particularly those of the Kiangsi soviet period. After 1926–27 the peasants were no longer left on their own; their ideology and their action were progressively transformed by contact with the militants and their ideas. The specifically negative characteristics of the peasantry were not sufficiently strong to form a durable obstacle to the fusion of the peasant movement and the Communist revolution. On the contrary, once the new Communist strategy of armed struggle was defined, the peasantry found itself in a concretely privileged position, not in Fanon's sense as a class somehow privileged by nature, but because

63, 64 In what was once a rent collection courtyard in Szechuan, a series of lifesize clay figures vividly recalls the landlords' exploitation of the peasants. The two scenes shown here depict, left, peasants bringing produce to their landlord and, above, an old peasant counting his grain.

there was now a peasant-orientated strategy, though one in which the peasantry did not have the initiative. From the moment when the revolutionaries from the towns decided on a long-term armed struggle, from 'red bases' which were both marginal in relation to the political centres of the country and geographically limited, it became indispensable to place the main revolutionary task in the hands of the peasants. Moreover, due to their social situation, they were better placed than the working class to make a contribution to the revolutionary process in the particular and temporary conditions imposed by this strategy.

The working-class movement in the cities has been capable, in Paris, Berlin, Petrograd, Moscow and Shanghai, for instance, of decisive revolutionary uprisings; but the urban environment leaves the worker highly dependent, from a material point of view, upon the modern social machinery. The worker can only free himself from this dependence for very short periods; so it is necessary for him to win the battle in a few days, or even hours. The peasant, on the other hand, still lives in a semi-natural environment; he is still, to some extent at least, a direct producer and retains a certain self-sufficiency, in food, heating and the means of producing primary necessities for survival. This is particularly true of peasants who live in the more backward areas, which are less dependent upon the modern market and on commodities from the towns. These are precisely those regions which, from a military point of view, are most suited to a prolonged armed struggle – such as the 'border regions' in wooded and mountainous inter-provincial confines, only tenuously controlled by the authorities in the plains.

The essential contribution of what we may for convenience call 'Maoism' does not lie in a modification of revolutionary theory; it does not see the peasantry as a revolutionary class endowed with an absolute, semi-messianic 'Mandate'. It does not question the ultimate subordination of the peasantry to those modern historical forces which alone are capable of leading the revolution to victory – socialist ideology and the Communist Party, both born of industrial society. The fundamental innovation of Mao Tse-tung lay in the almost *physical* discovery, rather than a mere theoretical appreciation, of the immense revolutionary potentialities of the peasantry in a great underdeveloped country like China. For him the peasantry was no longer a simple ally of the revolutionary forces, as Lenin had still seen it, an ally continually to be led, supervised and kept in a subordinate role. The peasantry was to be an integral part of the revolutionary movement, and a vital part of it – the armed struggle – was entrusted to them. Mao Tse-tung wrote in 1939:

> Since China's key cities have long been occupied by the powerful imperialists and their reactionary Chinese allies, it is imperative for the revolutionary ranks to turn the backward villages into advanced, consolidated base areas, into great military, political, economic and cultural bastions of the revolution from which to fight their vicious enemies who are using the cities for attacks on the rural districts, and in this way gradually to achieve the complete victory of the revolution through protracted fighting....

The same idea was taken up by Lin Piao in his speech of September 1965 entitled 'Long Live the Victory of the People's War':

> It was essential to rely mainly on the peasants if the people's war was to be won.... In the period of the War of Resistance against Japan, Comrade Mao Tse-tung again stressed that the peasants were the most reliable and most numerous ally of the proletariat and constituted the main force in the War of Resistance. The peasants were the main source of manpower for China's armies. The funds and supplies needed for a protracted war came chiefly from the peasants. In the anti-Japanese war it was imperative to rely mainly on the peasants and to arouse them to participate in the war on the broadest scale.
>
> The War of Resistance against Japan was in essence a peasant revolutionary war led by our Party.... To rely on the peasants, build rural base areas and use the countryside to encircle and finally capture the cities – such was the way to victory in the Chinese revolution.

The Chinese peasants played a vital role in the revolution, but they could only do so by adapting their struggles to general political

65 A commemorative painting shows Mao Tse-tung announcing the foundation of
the People's Republic of China at the Gate of the Heavenly Peace, in Peking,

1 October 1949. Chou En-lai, the Republic's first Foreign Minister and Premier, stands second from the left in the front row, in a grey uniform.

objectives. The age-old struggle of the peasants against the landlords was never given up; it never lost its elemental and visceral character; but it could no longer remain unrelated to the overall political situation. At every stage of the agrarian revolution and the peasant movement of the twentieth century, these general political objectives took priority.

We have seen, for example, that the Peasant Associations of 1926–27 had a very moderate agrarian programme, which called not for the redistribution of land, but only for control of rent and interest rates. As Mao Tse-tung pointed out in his Hunan report of January 1927, the important thing was the remarkable political dynamism demonstrated by the Peasant Associations. The 'fourteen great achievements' which he listed were of a political nature: over-throwing the political power of the county magistrate, humiliating the landlords and destroying their political ascendancy, destruction of the landlords' private militia and administration of the social and cultural affairs of the villages by peasants rather than 'Confucian' notables. The movement aimed first of all at the political and moral liberation of the peasants, without which it would have been fruitless to propose a radical reform of the system of economic exploitation.

In the liberated areas during the war against Japan the same precedence was still given to the political aspects of rural life. The policy of a 'united front for national salvation' was formulated, which invited the cooperation of 'enlightened landlords'. The radical measures for immediate division of land, which had been put in force in the Kiangsi soviet period, were temporarily shelved. This was no capitulation to the feudal system, it was not an opportunistic decision which sacrificed the interests of the class struggle against the landlords for some abstract concept of national interest. The more the peasants were mobilized politically against the Japanese, bearing the main brunt of the struggle in the guerilla bases behind enemy lines, the better were they consolidated and trained for war. The inequality which had always existed between peasants and landlords was *ipso facto* modified in favour of the peasants. The apparently 'rightist' agrarian policy of the years between 1937 and 1945 in the liberated areas was a direct preparation for the explosion of 1945–47 and the agrarian revolution. When this explosion came it was no longer a question of administrative measures of an economic nature; the task was once again the violent reversal of the peasants' political subordination to the landlords. The peasants had to be taught disrespect. Economic actions aimed at ending feudal exploitation and feudal land ownership were indispensable, but they had no chance of success unless the fundamental relations of dependence were torn apart by mass struggle.

The Chinese peasant movement was integrated with the modern revolutionary process, but it did not lose all its traditional traits. Because of the size of the country and the unequal development of political structures from region to region, the peasant movement continued to show marked geographical disparities. Within one province or between several provinces, the mountainous border regions continued to offer, as they had done in the past, a particularly favourable field of action for peasant struggles. The isolated and backward area of Ching-kang-shan, on the border between Hunan and Kiangsi, where Mao Tse-tung set up a base in 1927, was such a region. The anti-Japanese guerilla bases were located in similar terrain, like those of the Nien and the Black Flags a century earlier.

The geopolitical shift of the peasant movement from the south to the north is less of a traditional phenomenon; it marked a dividing line in time between the peasant movement of the twentieth century and the peasant struggles of past centuries, and reflected the close connection which now existed between the peasant movement and the overall political situation in China. The Peasant Association movement of the 'twenties was particularly strong in the south, in those regions through which the Canton revolutionary army had passed. The northern province of Honan is the exception which proves the rule: here Peasant Associations were also numerous because the local warlord regime of the 'Christian General' Feng Yü-hsiang was favourable to the Canton nationalists. The Chinese soviets of 1927-35 were also located in the south, and owed their existence, as Mao Tse-tung underlined in his article, *Why Is It That Red Political Power Can Exist in China?*, to the political experience which the peasants of these regions had acquired during the civil war of 1926–27. The two phases of the peasant struggle, before and after 1927, were characterized by very different political strategies: cooperation between the Communists and the Kuomintang in the first period and war between them in the second. But the geographical location was the same, since the second stemmed from the first and drew on the experience gained in it.

The Long March (1934–35) and the imminent Japanese invasion brought about an abrupt reversal of the geopolitical roles of the north and the south. It was the result of the defeat of the peasant soviets in the south by Kuomintang armies, but it led the Communists to take up an excellent strategic position in the north, within striking distance of the Japanese military bases. The Japanese invasion thus transferred the role of advance guard in the agrarian revolution from the peasants of the south to those of the north – a role which they kept even after the defeat of the Japanese. Just as the Chinese soviets had profited from the lessons of 1926–27, so the peasants of north China, in their struggle against the Kuomintang after 1945, had the advantage of the experience they had gained in the war of resistance against Japan. The strategy was again very different. After the defeat of Japan the whole effort was put into the class struggle against the Kuomintang and the forces in Chinese society which supported it. The agrarian revolution, postponed during the war, was renewed sharply in 1946; but the battlefield was the same – the border regions of north China. The peasants of the guerilla bases had acquired a fighting ability and a dynamism which enabled them to strike decisive blows against the Kuomintang. Although victory came in 1949, the political and military struggle had not everywhere reached the same level. The familiar phenomenon of unequal development in the peasant movement in different parts of the country was part of the heritage of the past, and was reflected in the use in People's China of the terms 'old liberated areas' and 'new liberated areas'.

The peasant movement, in its modern revolutionary form, had been given impetus by historical forces from the towns. It was twenty-two years before it came back to the towns, before it seized

66 'Advance under Mao Tse-tung's victorious banner!' A poster proclaims popular support for Mao's leadership.

the nerve centres of enemy power and established its own power and set to work, together with the other revolutionary forces in Chinese society, to construct a new China. For twenty-two years the peasant movement had been more or less cut off from the towns. The *Selected Works of Mao Tse-tung*, the official foundation of Chinese Communist historiography, have hardly any references to the underground struggles of workers, intellectuals and petit-bourgeoisie in the great urban centres occupied by the Japanese and the Kuomintang between 1927 and 1949. Was this isolation and this apparent lack of interest a question of principle, an expression of a fundamental

163

scepticism (which Fanon was later to develop into a theory) about the revolutionary contribution of towns in a country like China? Or was it rather the consequence of the profound divisions which existed from this time within the leadership of the Chinese Communist Party? The underground network, which the Communists were able to maintain in the towns in spite of the Japanese and the Kuomintang, was controlled by men who were at the time, or have since become, the adversaries of Mao Tse-tung, men like Li Li-san, Wang Ming and Liu Shao-ch'i. The opposition during the Cultural Revolution between Mao Tse-tung and Lin Piao on one side and Liu Shao-ch'i, P'eng Chen and others, had ancient roots. Mao and Lin were veterans of Yenan, leaders of the 'red bases', whereas the other group was composed of former leaders of the underground struggle in the 'white' regions. It is clear that the relative passivity of the Chinese towns at the time of the peasant revolution was essentially the result of circumstances, rather than of a deliberate decision.

The case of Vietnam gives an antithetic illustration of this hypothesis. The Communists of South Vietnam employ a general strategy of the 'Chinese' pattern, in the sense that the bases of the protracted struggle are in the countryside and the peasants provide the main effort. But the towns and the urban population – proletariat, intelligentsia and middle classes – play a more important role in the political and military struggle of South Vietnam against the American occupation than was the case in China thirty years earlier. Strikes, student demonstrations, commando operations against American military bases, large-scale politico-military actions such as that of Têt 1968, are carefully coordinated with the armed struggle in the countryside and mountains of South Vietnam. So a 'Chinese' strategy does not necessarily imply a lack of interest in the urban struggle. The revolutionary leadership in South Vietnam has not suffered the same kind of split as occurred in the Chinese Communist leadership between 1930 and 1940; it does not have the same practical reasons as Mao Tse-tung had to neglect revolutionary activity in the towns.

The tradition of Yenan as the peasant fortress of the Chinese revolution, the heroic image of the partisans of the 'old liberated areas', the long detour through the countryside which the revolution had to make before returning to the towns – in a word, the whole of this peasant heritage, gave a characteristic flavour to Chinese society after 1949. One might almost say that the great political crises of People's China, the great ideological debates, the conflicts over tendencies and political lines, revolve around the problems posed by this peasant heritage. Some Chinese leaders tended to turn their backs on it, and rather mechanically looked to the Soviet model for the construction of socialism; they favoured duality in state and party apparatus, gave precedence to modern technology and particularly to heavy industry, to slow development by Five-Year Plans controlled by learned economists; they wanted a tightly structured army with showy insignia and honorific distinctions. Such men, notably Liu Shao-ch'i, directed the affairs of China at the time of the first Five-Year Plan (1952–57) and to a certain extent again in 1962–65. The men of the opposing trend, grouped around Mao Tse-tung, attempted to repeat and perpetuate, in the period of construction, that kind of originality which had proved so fruitful after 1927, when they transferred the revolutionary centre of gravity to the Chinese countryside. They insist upon the role of the popular masses in public life, on the necessity of giving no permanent monopoly to the Party apparatus and the establishment. They demand that the economy should 'walk on two legs' and that it should have as much confidence in traditional methods as in modern technology. They insist that agriculture should be the base of the economy and industry its 'directing force'. They attempted, in 1958–59 for instance, to abandon the rigid centralized methods of the Five-Year Plans in favour of development by 'great leaps forward'. They demanded that people should be both 'red and expert', that priority be given to political mobilization of the masses rather than to pure technique. They tried to preserve the same intimate links between the army and the population as had existed during the Yenan period. With the Cultural Revolution this trend seems finally to have triumphed – at the cost of some compromise with the centrist, 'managerial' trend. It was the protagonists of the radical line who, in 1958–59, had pushed forward the development of the people's communes. These, and the Cultural Revolution itself, can be seen as a partial return to the Yenan model of 'revolutionary society', with its essentially peasant environment.

It is clear, however, that this peasant heritage alone cannot solve all the problems which a great modern state faces in the second half of the twentieth century. People's China is consequently obliged to master nuclear technology, to participate in international diplomatic conferences, to develop brain surgery and to work out very complex methods of economic administration. On the one hand, China faces up to the exigencies of modern life; at the same time she attempts to preserve the purity of her Marxist and peasant revolutionary heritage. Will this be possible?

Bibliography

BACKGROUND

L. Bianco, *Les origines de la révolution chinoise* (Paris 1967).

Jean Chesneaux, *L'Asie orientale aux XIXe et XXe siècles* (Paris 1966).

Jean Chesneaux and Marianne Bastid, *La Chine, des guerres de l'opium à la guerre franco-chinoise, 1840–1885* (Paris 1969).

J.K. Fairbank, E.O. Reischauer and A.M. Craig, *East Asia: The Modern Transformation* (Cambridge Mass. 1961).

A. Feuerwerker and S. Cheng, *Chinese Studies of Modern Chinese History* (Cambridge Mass. 1961).

Han Su-yin, *The Crippled Tree* (London 1965).

——, *A Mortal Flower* (London 1966).

——, *A Birdless Summer* (London 1968).

Ho Kan-chih, *A History of the Modern Chinese Revolution* (Peking 1960).

B.I. Schwartz, *Chinese Communism and the Rise of Mao* (Harvard 1951).

THE PEASANT CONDITION

Chen Han-seng, 'The burdens of the Chinese peasantry' in *Pacific Affairs* October 1921.

Chen Po-ta, *A Study of Land Rent in Pre-liberation China* (Peking 1958).

Fei Hsiao-tung, *Peasant Life in China* (London 1939).

Fei Hsiao-tung and Chang Chih-i, *Earthbound China* (Chicago 1947).

J. Hutson, 'Chinese life in the Tibetan foothills' in *New China Review* February 1920.

Institute of Pacific Relations, *Agrarian China, Selected Source Materials from Chinese Authors* (London 1939).

W. H. Mallory, *China, Land of Famine* (New York 1926).

R. H. Tawney, *Land and Labour in China* (London 1932).

THE PEASANT MOVEMENT BEFORE 1840

J. W. Dardess, 'The transformation of messianic revolt and the founding of the Ming Dynasty' in *Journal of Asian Studies* May 1970, pp. 539–58.

B. Favre, *Les sociétés secrètes en Chine* (Paris 1933).

J. P. Harrison, *The Communists and Chinese Peasant Rebellions* (New York 1969).

——, 'Communist interpretations of Chinese peasant wars' in *China Quarterly* October 1965.

Yuji Muramatsu, 'Some themes in Chinese rebel ideologies' in A. F. Wright (ed.), *The Confucian Persuasion* (Stanford 1960), pp. 241–68.

J. B. Parsons, 'The culmination of a Chinese peasant rebellion: Chang Hsien-chung in Szechuan 1644–46' in *Journal of Asian Studies* May 1957, pp. 387–400.

Paul Pelliot, 'La secte du Lotus Blanc et la secte du Nuage Blanc' in *Bulletin de l'école française de l'extrême Orient* 1903.

THE PEASANT MOVEMENT, 1840–1920

Fei-ling Blackburn, *Role and Organization of Chinese Secret Societies in the Late Ch'ing* (unpublished M.Phil. thesis, University of London 1968).

L. Brine, *The Taeping Rebellion in China* (London 1862).

J. M. Callery and M. Yvan, *History of the Insurrection in China* (London 1853).

Chen Han-seng, *Landlord and Peasant, A Study of the Agrarian Crisis in South China* (New York 1936).

Jerome Ch'en, 'The nature and characteristics of the Boxer movement: a morphological study' in *Bulletin of the School of Oriental and African Studies* 1960.

Jean Chesneaux, *Secret Societies in China: in the Nineteenth and Twentieth Centuries* (Michigan 1971, London 1972).

Jean Chesneaux, F. Davis and Nguyen Nguyet Ho (edd.), *Mouvements populaires et sociétés secrètes en Chine aux XIXe et XXe siècles* (Paris 1970).

Chiang Siang-tseh, *The Nien Rebellion* (Seattle 1955).

G. Dunstheimer, 'Religion et magie dans le mouvement des Boxeurs' in *T'oung Pao* 1959.

——, 'Le mouvement des Boxeurs: documents et études publiés depuis la deuxième guerre mondiale' in *Revue Historique* April 1964.

C. L. Geoffrey, 'The Red Spears in China' in *The China Weekly Review* 19 March 1927.

Theodore Hamberg, *The Visions of Hung Siu-tshuen and Origin of the Kwangsi Insurrection* (Hong Kong 1854).

Hsiao Kung-chuan, *Rural China, Imperial Control in the Nineteenth Century* (Seattle 1960).

Laai Yi-faai, *The Part Played by the Pirates of Kwangtung and Kwangsi Provinces in the T'ai-p'ing Insurrection* (unpublished Ph.D. thesis, University of California 1950).

T. T. Meadows, *The Chinese and their Rebellions* (London 1856).

Franz Michael, *The Taiping Rebellion* (Seattle 1966).

Yuji Muramatsu, 'The Boxers in 1898–99' in *Annals of the Hitosubashi Academy* April 1956.

F. Mury, 'Un mois en Mandchourie avec les Hounhouses' in *Le Tour du Monde* 1912.

D. H. Porter, 'Secret Societies in Shantung' in *The Chinese Recorder* 1886.

V. Purcell, *The Boxer Uprising, a Background Study* (Cambridge 1963).

Vincent Y. C. Shih, *The Taiping Ideology* (Seattle 1967).

Teng Ssu-yü, *The Nien Army and their Guerilla Warfare, 1858–1868* (Paris and The Hague 1961).

——, 'A political interpretation of Chinese rebellions and revolution' in *Tsinghua Journal of Chinese Studies* September 1958.

A. Ular, 'L'épopée communiste des proscrits mandchouriens' in *Revue Blanche* 1901.

Frederic Wakeman, *Strangers at the Gate: Social Disorder in South China, 1839–1861* (Berkeley 1966).

THE PEASANT MOVEMENT AND THE COMMUNIST REVOLUTION

Hamza Alavi, 'Peasants and Revolution' in *The Socialist Register* 1965.

A.J. Baxe, 'Some secret societies of Szechuan' in *Journal of the West China Border Research Society* 1936.

Jack Belden, *China Shakes the World* (London 1950).

L. Bianco, 'Les paysans et la révolution: Chine 1919–1949' in *Politique Étrangère* (Paris 1968).

Chen Po-ta, *Notes on Mao Tse-tung's 'Report of an Investigation into the Peasant Movement in Hunan'* (Peking 1954).

Jerome Ch'en, *Mao and the Chinese Revolution* (London 1965).

David and Isabel Crook, *Revolution in a Chinese Village* (London 1959).

Harrison Forman, *Report from Red China* (New York 1945).

J. Guillermaz, 'La politique agraire du parti communiste chinois' in *Revue Militaire d'Information* July 1960.

R.M. Hofheinz, *The Peasant Movement and Rural Revolution: Communists in the Countryside, 1923–1927* (unpublished Ph.D. thesis, Harvard University 1966).

H.J. Howard, *Ten Weeks with Chinese Bandits* (London 1927).

Harold Isaacs, *The Tragedy of the Chinese Revolution* (Stanford 1961).

Chalmers A. Johnson, *Peasant Nationalism and Communist Power* (Stanford 1962).

Bela Kun, *Räte China: Dokumente des Chinesischen Revolution* (Moscow 1934).

J.D.M. Lamb, *Development of the Agrarian Movement and Agrarian Legislation in China, 1912–1930* (Peking 1931).

Liao T'ai-ch'u, 'The Ko-lao-hui in Szechuan' in *Pacific Affairs* June 1947.

Miao Min, *Fang Tche-min, sa vie et ses combats* (Peking 1960).

Mao Tse-tung, *Selected Works*, 4 vols. (Peking 1961).

R. W. McColl, 'The Oyuwan Soviet Area, 1927–1933' in *Journal of Asian Studies* November 1967.

J. E. Rue, *Mao Tse-tung in Opposition, 1927–1935* (Stanford 1966).

S. R. Schram, *The Political Thought of Mao Tse-tung* (Harmondsworth 1969).

Eto Shinkichi, 'Hailufeng, the first Chinese soviet government' in *China Quarterly* October 1961 and January 1962.

Agnes Smedley, *The Great Road, The Life and Times of Chu Teh* (New York 1956).

——, *The Battle Hymn of China* (New York 1943).

Edgar Snow, *Red Star over China* (New York 1937).

G. Stein, *The Challenge of Red China* (London 1945).

Shanti Swarup, *A Study of the Chinese Communist Movement, 1927–34* (Oxford 1966).

E. R. Wolf, *Peasant Wars of the Twentieth Century* (New York 1969).

V. Yakhontoff, *The Chinese Soviets* (New York 1934).

THE PEASANTRY AND PEOPLE'S CHINA

Chao Kuo-chün, *Agricultural Development and Problems in China Today. A Survey of Chinese Communist Agrarian Policy* (New Delhi 1958).

Chao Shu-li, *Changes in Li Village* (Peking 1950).

——, *The Rhymes of Li Yu-tsai* (Peking 1954).

R. Dumont, *Révolution dans les campagnes Chinoises* (Paris 1956).

W. Hinton, *Fanshen, a Documentary of Revolution in a Chinese Village* (New York 1966).

Jan Myrdal, *Report from a Chinese Village* (New York and London 1965).

C. K. Yang, *A Chinese Village in Early Communist Transition* (Cambridge Mass. 1959).

Yuan Tung-li, *Social Development of Modern China* (New Haven 1956).

The Rising Tide of Socialist Upsurge in the Chinese Countryside (Peking 1955) with a preface by Mao Tse-tung.

List of Illustrations

1 Map of China. Drawn by David Eccles.

2 'Umbrella' house in Amoy belonging to a clan, c. 1910.

3 Beggars, 1874. Photo: Radio Times Hulton Picture Library.

4 Hung Hsiu-ch'üan; pen and ink drawing from J. M. Callery and M. Yvan, *History of the Insurrection in China*, 1853.

5 Taiping army going into action; lithograph from Lin-le, *Ti-Ping Tien-kwoh*, 1866.

6, 7 Imprints of the state seal of the Taiping Heavenly Kingdom; illustration from *Chung-kuo chin-tai-shih ts'an-k'ao p'u-pien chi*, 1958.

8 Taiping leaders; late nineteenth-century print. Photo: Zoltan Wegner.

9 Imperial troops attack Nanking, 1864; facsimile of contemporary engraving. Photo: Roger Viollet.

10, 11 Illustrations from a modern book on the Nien rebellion. Patrick Destenay collection.

12 Official seal of a commander of the Moslem rebellion in Yunnan (1853–73); illustration from *Chung-kuo chin-tai-shih ts'an-k'ao p'u-pien chi*, 1958.

13 *The Miracle Teapot*; Russian cartoon, c. 1901. Church Missionary Society.

14 *The God of Thunder Destroying the Pigs and the Goat*, from a series of popular woodcuts. Church Missionary Society. Photo: Zoltan Wegner.

15 *Shooting the Pig and Decapitating the Sheep*, from a series of popular woodcuts. Church Missionary Society. Photo: Zoltan Wegner.

16 Name-plate of the Mining Department of the Shantung Railway Company, 1898; illustration from *Chung-kuo chin-tai-shih ts'an-k'ao p'u-pien chi*, 1958.

17 An American police-station in Peking, 1902. Photo: G. Sirot.

18 Engraving of the British Factory, Canton, 18 March 1843. Photo: Radio Times Hulton Picture Library.

19 Deaconess Ellen Mort of the Fukien Mission, c. 1900. Church Missionary Society.

20 Dragon-pearl banner of the Boxer movement, discovered in Shanghai, 1957; illustration from *Chung-kuo chin-tai-shih ts'an-k'ao p'u-pien chi*, 1958.

21 Boxer banner bearing the inscription 'Support the Ch'ing, destroy the foreigner'; illustration from *Chung-kuo chin-tai-shih ts'an-k'ao p'u-pien chi*, 1958.

22 Pen and ink sketch of a Boxer from a secondary school textbook published in 1964. Patrick Destenay collection.

23 Woodcut showing starving peasants seizing grain from a landlord, April 1910; illustration from *Chung-kuo chin-tai-shih ts'an-k'ao p'u-pien chi*, 1958.

24 Sun Yat-sen. Photo: Camera Press.

25 Sun Yat-sen and members of his government, Nanking, 1912. Photo: Camera Press.

26–29 Coins struck by the Chin Ch'ien society to denote membership; illustration from *Chung-kuo chin-tai-shih ts'an-k'ao p'u-pien chi*, 1958.

30 German cartoon on Western intervention in China; late nineteenth century. Photo: Roger Viollet.

31 Victims of famine, July 1930. Photo: Radio Times Hulton Picture Library.

32 Execution squad in Shanghai, February 1927. Photo: Paul Popper.

33 British sailors from H.M.S. *Hawkins* in Shanghai, March 1927. Photo: Paul Popper.

34 Chiang Kai-shek and Wang Ching-wei, Canton, November 1925. Photo: Radio Times Hulton Picture Library.

35 Membership card of the Peasant Association of Lu-feng, 1929; illustration from *Museum of the Peasant Movement Institute directed by Mao Tse-tung*, 1959. Patrick Destenay collection.

36 Membership card of a Peasant Association of Canton province, 1925; illustration from *Museum of the Peasant Movement Institute directed by Mao Tse-tung*, 1959. Patrick Destenay collection.

37 Russian poster advocating support for China, 1931. Kunstgewerbemuseum, Zurich.

38 Badge of the special committee of the Chinese Communist Party in T'ung-ch'iang; illustration from *Museum of the Peasant Movement Institute directed by Mao Tse-tung*, 1959. Patrick Destenay collection.

39 Sun Yat-sen with Blücher and Mamaev, Canton, autumn 1924. Photo: Novosti Press Agency.

40 Mao Tse-tung. Photo: Paul Popper.

41 *Support for the People's Very Own Army*; woodcut, 1940s.

42 Landlord; woodcut from a series made 1931–36.

43 *Over the Mountain*; painting by Ai-Chung Hsin, 1957. Centre Culturel Chinois, Paris. Photo: Snark International.

44 *The Hanging Bridge*; pencil sketch made on the Long March.

45 *Through the Mountains*; pencil sketch made on the Long March.

Index

Numbers in italic refer to illustrations

missionaries 25, *49*, 51, 55; Catholic 47, 56; Protestant 30, 47
Mongols 21, 28
Moslem rebellions 23, 36–7, 38
Münzner, Thomas 7

Nan-ch'ang 101, 105, 113
Nanking 25, 30, 31, *32*, 33, 38, 60, 71, 75, 85, 86, 122, 140; Treaty of (1842) 23
Nan-t'ung 78
National Peasant Congress 99
Needham, Joseph 11
New Army 59, 61, 120
New Fourth Army 127
New Testament 29
New York Times 135
Nien rebellion 23, 32–6, 37, 38, 44, 55, 66, 67, 69, 70, 71, 76, 77, 161
Ninghsia 62, 105, 123, 132, 140
Northern Expedition 90, 99

Okamura, General 122
Old Testament 29
On New Democracy 126
Opium Wars 23, 31, 65, 74
orphanages, Catholic 51
'O-yü-wan' base 104

Pacific Ocean 80
Pai Lang, peasant leader 63
Paoting 140
Paris 104, 156
Peace Maintenance Committee 122
Peasant Associations 90, 92–5, 98, 100, 101, 105, 109, 160, 161
Peasant Movement Training Institute 95
Peasant Nationalism and Communist Power 127
Peking 30, 31, 33, 40, *48*, 50, 55, 62, 63, 67, *123*, 140; siege of 74
P'eng Chen 164
P'eng P'ai, Communist leader 94
People's Republic of China 19, 148, 149
Petrograd 104, 156
Philippines 80
p'ing-chün (Equality) 14
P'ing-liu-li revolt 68

P'ing-shan 59
Poor Peasants' Association 145
Poor Peasants' Union 152
population: explosion of in nineteenth century 11, 14, 23; movement of 40
production campaigns 132
purification campaign 146–7

Razin, Stenka 7
Red Army (Chinese) 102, 103, *106*, 107, 111, 117, 139, 152
Red Band 38
Red Beards (Hung-hu-tzu) 50, 59, 60, 67, 68, 69, 76
Red Eye-brows 7
Red Spears (*Hung ch'iang Hui*) 69, 84–5, 94, 152
Red Turban rebellion 38, 75, 77, 111
removal of the Mandate *see* Mandate
republicanism 57, 59; republican revolution (1911) 60–4, 75, 78
Revolution in a Chinese Village 141
revolution (1924–7) 85, 90, 93, 99, 100
Rhenish peasants 16
Rhymes of Li Yu-tsai, The 138
'rice Christians' 51
rice cultivation 10
Righteous and Harmonious Fists 17; *see also* Boxers
Rockefeller family 86
Russia 7, 50, 76, 104; soviets in 102

Saint Paul 145
salt: price of 56; smuggling 18, 32, 34, 36, 71
Sanko Seisaku ('three alls') 122
San-yuan-li incident 50, 51
secret societies 14, 17, 23, 25, 37, 38, 41, 44, 51, 57, 59, 60, 63, 67, 72, 75, 83, 84, 85, 86, 89, 95, 101, 111, 117, 152; feminism within 18, 52, 136
Seng-ko-lin-ch'in, Mongol commander 36
Shanghai 46, 60, 79, 80, *88*, 95, 99, 101, 104, 108, 113, 148, 151
Shan-Kang 111
Shansi 63, 85, 123, 132, 133